I0138347

Movies to See before You Graduate from High School

Movies to See before You Graduate from High School

Michael Howarth

Rowman & Littlefield
Lanham • Boulder • New York • London

Published by Rowman & Littlefield
An imprint of The Rowman & Littlefield Publishing Group, Inc.
4501 Forbes Boulevard, Suite 200, Lanham, Maryland 20706
www.rowman.com

6 Tinworth Street, London, SE11 5AL, United Kingdom

British Library Cataloguing in Publication Information Available

Library of Congress Cataloging-in-Publication Data

Names: Howarth, Michael, 1977– author.
Title: Movies to see before you graduate from high school / Michael Howarth.
Description: Lanham : Rowman & Littlefield, [2020] | Includes bibliographical references and index. | Summary: "From Almost Famous to Whale Rider, this is a fun look at 60 films that best define what it means to be an adolescent. Each entry identifies the genre, provides a brief plot summary, lists the key themes, and explains why the film is an essential viewing for teens everywhere"— Provided by publisher.
Identifiers: LCCN 2019018723 (print) | LCCN 2019980294 (ebook) | ISBN 9781538120019 (cloth) | ISBN 9781538120026 (ebook)
Subjects: LCSH: Coming-of-age films—Bibliography.
Classification: LCC PN1995.9.Y6 H69 2020 (print) | LCC PN1995.9.Y6 (ebook) | DDC 791.43/65235—dc23
LC record available at https://lccn.loc.gov/2019018723
LC ebook record available at https://lccn.loc.gov/2019980294

CONTENTS

CONGRATULATIONS, CLASS OF . . . SENIOR SUPERLATIVES

An Almost Introduction

Most Opinionated

Coming-of-age films have always been, and will always be, popular because they exemplify the high school experience: four wild years filled with pep rallies and nosy parents, awkward first dates, lockers that smell of dirty gym socks, and hallways filled with bone-crushing rejection. Adolescence is an important period of our lives because it wraps up our childhood while preparing us for adulthood. The films that define those teenage years are often a blueprint for how to survive the high school experience. Put simply, watching a coming-of-age film is like having a heartfelt conversation with someone who understands completely all of the drama and craziness we're going through on a daily basis.

This book is a selection of sixty coming-of-age films that are essential viewing. They remind me of a time in my life when I had many hopes and few responsibilities. They force me to understand not only who I once was, but how the decisions I made as a teenager have helped to shape who I am now. These sixty films roam the cinematic landscape—everything from comedy and horror to foreign language and animation. They appeal to a wide range of personalities. And while they differ in their moods, settings, and characters, they are all honest and fearless in their presentation of characters who grapple with many of the themes and conflicts that have always been such an integral part of growing up: depression, bullying, jealousy, or trust, to name a few. Each film also includes a recommended double feature for those nights when hanging out with one friend just isn't enough.

Best Personality

Adolescence is that tumultuous stretch of time between the ages of twelve and twenty. It's an important stage when we begin to make critical choices—regardless of whether those choices are inspired, hasty, heartfelt, or stupid—and when we begin to establish a sense of our own independence, separate from our parents and teachers. But adolescence is also a time filled with harsh realizations. We come to understand that life is not always fair, and that sometimes it can just plain suck, like when our parents ground us for the weekend because we failed an exam or missed a curfew. The best coming-of-age films have their own distinct flavor, and they don't easily fall into one simple category, like a comedy or a drama. They're a mixture of humor and pathos, of laughing and crying, of lamenting and celebrating. They share life lessons and poignant advice in ways that never seem condescending or cheesy but, instead, seem sincere and inspirational.

Most Likely to Succeed

Most teenagers want to be noticed, or at least respected by their peers. They want to feel included and treated as unique individuals who are separate from their parents. Many characters in coming-of-age films exhibit a strong desire to triumph and prove they're significant. This often occurs when the doubters are talking a lot of trash and the odds seem insurmountable. No one likes it when our abilities are questioned, especially when we're in the midst of establishing our own self-worth. The truth is, whether we're studying for tests or composing college essays, whether we're trying out for the varsity baseball team or running for senior class president, we want to feel proud of our accomplishments. And we want everyone else to acknowledge them, too.

Accomplishments in a coming-of-age film can range from securing a part-time job or dating the most beautiful girl in school to acing the final exam or standing up to a group of bullies. Regardless of how the victory is achieved, coming-of-age films applaud perseverance. They remind us that many people experience similar fears and conflicts, and they show us a path to success. They're not afraid to champion the underdog because it's an important role every one of us will play at some point during our lives.

Best Couple

Coming-of-age films usually contain a love story. But they're not always the happy and shiny version that we hope for, chock full of compliments and passionate kisses. Sometimes, they are heart wrenching and devastating and bursting with anger. It's never easy trying to share quality time between friends and a significant other. We must learn to organize and prioritize our time so we remain connected to each important part of our life, whether it's at home, at school, or out in the community. Engaging in an intimate relationship forces us to value our time in new ways. It's hard enough to share a locker with someone, let alone a few hours during a hectic week. Adolescent needs and responsibilities typically involve some combination of eating, sleeping, homework, extracurricular activities, and a part-time job.

Dating someone is one of the first steps in reaching adulthood. It's an opportunity to hone our communication skills and act selfless when necessary. It's a time when we learn how to process our own heartbreak, and also how to deliver it to others with delicacy and compassion. Coming-of-age films are blueprints for how to talk to the opposite sex without looking like a complete moron. They teach us how to navigate the eventual disagreements that plague every relationship. They also show us how to charm the most popular person in school so we can sit together in the cafeteria eating pizza cut into squares, or hold hands while marching down a sterile hallway flooded in fluorescent light.

Best Bromance

Coming-of-age films love to illustrate the importance of teamwork. They stress the idea that it's okay to ask for help because there are times when we all need it. This is why coming-of-age films often feature a best friend, or even a tight group of friends. The best friend can be an important supporter and confidant, offering advice to the main character and acting as the voice of reason. Or the best friend can be brash, spoiled, rude, immature, and unlikable. Sometimes, the best friend is simply weak and dependent. Either way, a best friend who is presented in a negative light shows us how unappealing those traits can appear to other people. Such undesirable characters also show us what kind of person the main character might become if he or she makes poor decisions and doesn't mature properly.

It's important to recognize the importance of close friendships because we tend to know ourselves better when we understand how our friends view us and respond to our actions. Oftentimes, our friends can provide an objective viewpoint, one that helps to put our surrounding world into a sharper focus by affording us a fresh perspective. If we consider the high school years as an epic journey filled with triumphs and fraught with dangers, then it makes sense that we would want a traveling companion to help ease the burdens and frustrations. We want someone to cheer us on as we trudge through the tangled undergrowth on our way toward independence and self-discovery.

Most Liked by Parents

In the best coming-of-age films, the teens are active decision-makers. They question their own motives and they puzzle through a series of predicaments, sometimes selfishly and sometimes naively. Yes, there are the typical choices that need to be made—which classes to take, whether to ask someone to the prom, or which new series to binge-watch on Netflix over the weekend—but adolescence is also a period filled with important decisions about money, relationships, and future plans. It's a transitory stage when we stop relying on our parents for everything and we begin to assume responsibility for our actions and their consequences, even if we'd rather not. To most teenagers, adults are supporting characters who love them but don't always understand them. These are the years when parents and their children argue about dating and curfews and part-time jobs. Teenagers believe their parents have no clue what it's like to grow up in the present time. And the parents, half-bemused and half-annoyed, wonder if their children are gaining the tools necessary to survive in the real world.

Because of this, the communication between teenagers and their parents is a vital component in coming-of-age films. Some stories present the parents as nurturing and encouraging. They let their children make mistakes so they can process and learn from those mistakes. Other stories present the parents as overly controlling. They have a debilitating effect on their child's growth and development. And some stories contain no parents at all, thus providing yet another perspective on the central role that parents can play in an adolescent's maturation process. While the quality of parenting clearly ranges from nonexistent to smothering, the best parents understand that their goal is to prepare their child to eventually leave home with intelligence and confidence, able to survive on his or her own.

Best Dressed

Teenagers have always been fascinated with pop culture. They're constantly tuned in to the newest fashions and technologies. They want to own the latest iPhone and gaming system. They want to use the newest slang and sound knowledgeable about the trendiest music and movies. They believe that if they look cool, then they will act cool, which will increase their social standing and propel them into glamorous parties and exclusive conversations. Appearance is incredibly important to teenagers because it reflects not only how they see themselves, but it affects how others view them. Pop culture, however, is continuously changing, from year to year and decade to decade. When we define the 1980s or the 1990s, we must discuss all aspects of pop culture that influenced that specific generation's attitudes and behaviors: cars, music, films, television, politics, sports, and fashions, just to name a few.

Part of the fun of watching coming-of-age films is seeing how they reflect the time period in which they are set, and how pop culture plays a key role in the characters' lives. Human nature doesn't change, whether involving the onset of sexual feelings, the desire to be liked, or the conflict between wanting to be an individual versus wanting to be part of a group. But the ways in which those emotions are triggered and expressed is often a product of pop culture. There has always been a valuable relationship between the adolescent and his or her environment, especially in regard to any accessories (clothes, books, posters, iPhones) that illustrate the adolescent's personality. Whether it's sporting the hottest designer jeans or cruising up and down Main Street in a brand-new car, the importance of pop culture on one's self-identity can't be underestimated.

Most Likely to Leave and Never Come Back

Many adolescents have a conflicted relationship with their environment. This conflict might stem from feeling trapped in a home with too many rules, or it might arise from having to juggle a part-time job with a lousy work ethic. On a broader scale, many adolescents speak of wanting to leave their hometown and explore the world, of feeling stagnant by backdrops that have become boring and predictable. These thoughts symbolize a growing need for independence, as well as a desire to create new memories that are separate from those experienced with the friends and parents who will always be connected to a unique place and time in our lives. It's not always easy to navigate the spaces around us, no matter how large or small or with whom we might have to share them, but being aware of our surroundings can remind us that physical space is always connected to our emotional state.

In coming-of-age films, the setting features prominently—whether it's a home, a school, or the local hangout—because it helps to define the characters and their assorted views on life. We need to pay attention to those places where the characters feel safe and secure, or where they feel threatened and vulnerable. We need to understand how certain settings influence a character's personal relationships, or how they compel the character to make a decisive choice that alters the mood of the entire film. As the characters evolve, so, too, will the locations they frequent. The high school years are defined by motion—by a burning desire to flee from the constraints of childhood and to charge headlong into the freedoms of adulthood—and the characters in a coming-of-age film are always trying to move forward in pursuit of something better.

Most Creative

One of the difficulties in being a teenager is toeing the line between being a leader and being a follower. There's a struggle between expressing ourselves as a unique individual while remaining part of a tight-knit group that understands and encourages us. There are lots of different groups floating around high schools, and the interests that bring people together can be anything from fashion and social status to artistic areas like music, literature, or film. It's not just our friends who help to define us and lend us some much-needed perspective, but also the songs we listen to, the novels we read, the movies we watch, and even the foods we eat. For better or worse, we are products of our own culture.

This book is just one of those tight-knit groups. The sixty films included herein are uplifting and hilarious. They are scary and sad. They are shocking and thought provoking. They are the films we discuss with our friends and lovers and parents. Their stories, and how they play out, make us question our own important decisions and rethink our own unique relationships. Ultimately, these films are like mirrors. We see bits and pieces of ourselves reflected on-screen, whether we're connecting with certain characters or reacting to certain situations. We become invested in these stories because they show us how we live our lives, or how we wish we could live our lives. Some of them are even cautionary tales that warn us about involving ourselves with certain types of people or engaging in specific behaviors.

Each of these films is a private conversation we can have with characters who will never judge us, with characters who will never yell at us, and with characters who will never tell us we're wrong because we act differently or because we hold certain principles. We rejoice when they succeed, and we feel bad when they fail. These sixty films—no matter how raucous or thrilling, no matter how heartrending or funny—can teach us important lessons about our relationships to the world, and about our relationships to each other. Because as playwright George Bernard Shaw famously remarked, "Life isn't about finding yourself. Life is about creating yourself."

ALMOST FAMOUS
(2000)

Directed by: Cameron Crowe
Written by: Cameron Crowe
Cast: Billy Crudup (Russell), Frances McDormand (Elaine), Kate Hudson (Penny Lane), Patrick Fugit (William), Philip Seymour Hoffman (Lester), Zooey Deschanel (Anita)
Rating: Rated R for language, drug content, and brief nudity
Runtime: 122 minutes
Genre: Comedy-drama

The Gist: This semiautobiographical film, based on Cameron Crowe's time as a music journalist, is set in San Diego in 1973. The story centers on William Miller, an unpopular fifteen-year-old who loves music and dreams of being a rock journalist. But his single mother, Elaine, is a college professor who hates rock and roll. She believes that type of music is all about sex and drugs. While she clearly loves her two children, her passionate views on music and pop culture clash with both of them. This is especially true in regard to William's older sister, Anita. Feeling frustrated and constrained, she leaves home to become a flight attendant. Before leaving, however, she instructs him to look under her bed for a secret stash of records.

William writes music reviews and articles for his high school newspaper. He is influenced by bands like Led Zeppelin, Deep Purple, and Humble Pie. Eventually, he befriends famous rock journalist Lester

Bangs. Lester is a larger-than-life personality who lives and breathes music. He understands the powerful ways that lyrics and melodies can influence our lives, and his dialogue is honest and poetic. He tells William that whenever he gets lonely he should just go to the record store and visit all of his friends. Lester eloquently describes the various connections between music and culture, and how one often influences the other.

Impressed by William's writing, Lester gives him an assignment to review a Black Sabbath concert. This is William's first paying job as a music journalist, and he approaches the task with pride. His mother is worried, but she allows him to attend the concert. There, he meets Penny Lane, a popular groupie for the band Stillwater. She is the most outspoken and quirky woman he has ever met, and he is immediately charmed by her smile and bubbly attitude. Over the course of the evening, William is captivated by the glitz and glamour and backstage revelry. He ends up bonding with several of the band members, especially Russell the lead guitarist.

Because of his Black Sabbath gig, William then receives a call from *Rolling Stone* magazine. Believing he is much older, the editors hire him to interview Stillwater, whose song "Fever Dog" has topped the charts. Thrilled at the invitation to write a feature article, William goes on tour

Philip Seymour Hoffman, Patrick Fugit. *DreamWorks/Photofest* © *DreamWorks*

with the band. Thus begins a series of humorous and poignant adventures in which he learns as much about himself as he does about other people. His travels take him from the West Coast to the East Coast, and to several cities in between. The time away from his overbearing mother provides several opportunities for William to grow on his own by making his own decisions and by enduring a few mistakes.

Lester warns William not to make friends with Stillwater. Of course, William doesn't listen because he's entranced by the rowdy poker games and the noisy get-togethers. He's spellbound by the rocking music and the cheering fans. He parties in hotel rooms and rides on the tour bus. At a party in Kansas, William gathers with a crowd of kids next to a pool while Russell, who is on acid, stands atop a roof to address a crowd of cheering fans. As a lonely high school student, William is fascinated by the fame and adoration surrounding Stillwater. He enjoys the attention showered upon him whenever he's in their presence.

Throughout the film, William witnesses countless romances and disagreements, as well as a series of resentments and lies. He learns that being part of a group—and having to depend on other people—is not always easy, and that it sometimes requires personal sacrifices. There are fights among the band members, but William also struggles with finding time to interview each of them. As his anxiety mounts, he wonders how he will organize his jumble of thoughts into a coherent article. When he calls Lester for advice, the colorful critic says he should tell *Rolling Stone* that the article is "a think piece about a midlevel band struggling with their own limitations in the harsh face of stardom." Lester's comments reflect the complicated dynamics that develop throughout the film. William falls for Penny Lane, but she is obsessed with the band and its music. Elaine needs to loosen her grip on William and understand that he's growing up and needs to be on his own.

The band calls William "the enemy" because they want to be cautious around him. They aren't sure what they can tell him, or what he might write about them. As rock stars, they're more concerned with looking cool to the public and to their fans than they are with having William accurately report on everything he sees during the tour. At the heart of the film, though, is the power of music to express emotions and to bring people together. Despite the drama, this is a feel-good movie about the ways in which music can define us. William's journey with Stillwater breaks him out of his comfort zone and helps him to feel included in a group for the first time in his life.

Why You Should See This Film: Because it's a musical odyssey involving rock stars, an aspiring journalist, and a cross-country tour filled with friendships and revelations.

Main Themes: Communication * Family * Jealousy * Ambition * Selfishness

Classic Line: "They don't even know what it is to be a fan. To truly love some silly little piece of music, or some band, so much that it hurts."

Recommended Double Feature: *Taking Woodstock* (2009); Rated R, 121 minutes, Drama-comedy

AMERICAN GRAFFITI

(1973)

Directed by: George Lucas
Written by: George Lucas, Gloria Katz, and Willard Huyck
Cast: Ron Howard (Steve), Richard Dreyfuss (Curt), Paul Le Mat (John Milner), Cindy Williams (Laurie), Charles Martin Smith (Toad), Candy Clark (Debbie), Mackenzie Phillips (Carol)
Rating: Rated PG for adult content and adult language
Runtime: 110 minutes
Genre: Comedy-drama

The Gist: This slice of life takes place over the course of one single night in Modesto, California, in 1962. Loaded with an awesome fifties soundtrack and a cast of colorful characters, it focuses on four friends: Curt, Steve, John Milner, and Toad. The film opens with a shot of Mel's Drive-In, a local hangout spot for the teenagers. The four friends meet there to plan the night's activities. In the morning, Curt and Steve will leave for college. Curt, however, admits to having second thoughts about leaving Modesto.

Each character has his own set of insecurities. Steve is dating Laurie—who is also Curt's sister—and while he claims to love her, he tells her that he wants to see other girls while he's away at college. Steve relishes the freedom of being on his own. Feeling emboldened, he tries to romance Laurie by suggesting that not being exclusive will strengthen their relationship. He tells her that only then will they know for sure if they are truly in love. Naturally, Laurie becomes upset at his request, and the young couple spend the rest of the evening arguing and making up.

Curt, on the other hand—and despite being awarded a two-thousand-dollar scholarship from the Moose Lodge—still feels a connection to his hometown. He's searching for something grand and wonderful, but he doesn't quite know what it is. He's excited and apprehensive about his uncertain future. And when Curt glimpses the woman of his dreams, a gorgeous blonde driving a white Thunderbird, he spends the rest of the film trying to find her. Later, he has a run-in with a gang called the Pharaohs, and the time he spends with them offers him a different perspective on his own situation.

Milner is the tough guy in the group, hassled by the police because he's always cruising the strip. He's popular and has a reputation for owning the coolest car. While trying to pick up girls, he is saddled with a sixteen-year-old named Carol. He's embarrassed to be seen with someone so young, and their bantering provides some of the film's funniest moments. In addition to Carol, Milner must contend with another drag racer who challenges him to a race on Paradise Road. Milner wants to maintain his status as the king of the town, but he worries about losing his edge. Another character echoes these concerns when he claims that Milner is getting old and isn't as fast as he used to be.

Toad, like Milner, is also staying in Modesto. He's a nerdy type who clearly looks up to his three close friends. Toad is thrilled when Steve loans him his car while he's away at school. Feeling like a hotshot, Toad drives up and down the street until he spots Debbie, a gorgeous blonde who likes his car and agrees to ride with him. Amazed that Debbie wants to hang out with him, Toad tries to impress her all night long. His escapades involve trying to purchase alcohol, getting into a fistfight, and retrieving Steve's car when it's stolen.

Throughout the film, there's a battle between teenagers wanting to hold on to the moment—to cling to youthful exuberance—and wanting to separate from everything that's familiar. Steve, who's the most eager to leave, thinks it would be terrible to remain seventeen forever. And Mr. Wolfe, an adult who's supervising the school dance, tells Curt that he should experience life and have some fun. The film presents characters teetering on the edge of adolescence and adulthood. They're constantly in motion, driven forward by optimism and a need to succeed. They just don't always know in which direction they should be going.

Wolfman Jack, the famous American disc jockey, plays himself in the film, and his radio broadcasts are interspersed throughout the story. They connect the various characters as they meet and separate over the course of several hours. This device ties the film together and illustrates the role that music plays in our lives. This is demonstrated when Curt visits Wolfman Jack in his quest to find his elusive blonde beauty and the Wolfman offers him some poignant advice.

American Graffiti explores relationships in different ways. There's the bond among best friends, the bond between lovers, and even the bond between an individual and his or her hometown. The film's successful blend of comedy and drama promotes the importance of love and friendship during this pivotal time in an adolescent's life. These characters like to talk—whether about themselves or to each other—and their dialogue is smart and funny and realistic.

Toward the end of the film, when Curt is on the phone with his mystery lady, he shouts, "You're the most beautiful, exciting thing I've ever seen in my life, and I don't know anything about you." In that moment, full of dreams and possibilities, he could be speaking for every teenager who contemplates, with an equal amount of fear and excitement, an uncertain future.

Why You Should See This Film: Because it's a rock-and-roll mosaic of small-town America in which a group of friends cruise around town in search of a good time.

Main Themes: Individuality * Disillusionment * Ambition * Fear * Selfishness

Classic Line: "It doesn't make sense to leave home to look for home."

Recommended Double Feature: *Breaking Away* (1979); Rated PG, 101 minutes, Comedy-drama

AMERICAN PIE
(1999)

Directed by: Paul Weitz
Written by: Adam Herz
Cast: Jason Biggs (Jim), Seann William Scott (Stifler), Chris Klein (Oz), Thomas Ian Nicholas (Kevin), Eddie Kaye Thomas (Finch), Eugene Levy (Mr. Levenstein)
Rating: Rated R for strong sexuality, crude sexual dialogue, language, drinking, and nudity
Runtime: 96 minutes
Genre: Comedy

The Gist: Four close friends attend East Great Falls High School where they move through the typical adolescent landscape involving parents, popularity, classes, and relationships. They party, hang out at a local restaurant, and ponder the future in a series of gross and humorous adventures. In addition, each character deals with his own personal issues, mostly centering on the opposite sex. *American Pie* is a time capsule of the 1990s, not only in the style of the fashion and in its portrayal of technology—despite the absence of cell phones, there is one classic scene involving a web camera—but also in the music, which is lively and energetic. The soundtrack features songs from groups like Tonic, Third Eye Blind, and Blink-182.

Paul Finch is a sophisticate who drinks mochaccinos and considers himself cultured. He runs home during the middle of the day to use the bathroom because he's afraid of the germs in a public restroom. His smoothness with the ladies is nonexistent, so he pays a female friend to spread some lies about both his stamina in bed and his toughness. These flattering rumors suddenly endear him to the female population at East Great Falls High School.

Then there's Kevin, a nerdy type who is dating a beautiful girl. They plan to stay together after they graduate, and the subject of when they should have sex is a major obstacle between them, leading to angry words and hurt feelings. Their relationship raises important questions about the validity of long-distance relationships and the tendency of high school students to plan for a future that is still unclear. It's Kevin who proposes that the four friends make a sacred pact to have sex before they graduate. Leaping onto the couch one morning, he proclaims they are all masters of their sexual destinies.

Jim Levenstein is the clumsy and inexperienced friend whose crazy antics provide some of the film's funniest moments. He has a crush on a foreign exchange student named Nadia. His attempts to flirt with her are awkward and hilarious, whether at a crowded keg party or in the privacy of his own bedroom. Jim feels so much pressure to have sex, and he is so

Jason Biggs, Shannon Elizabeth. *Universal Pictures/Photofest © Universal Pictures*

desperate to find a date for the prom, that he asks a "band camp geek" named Michelle to go with him.

It's clear that Jim is immature—like when he gushes about how hot Ariel looks in Disney's *The Little Mermaid*—but his dad, who is sweet and understanding, is a terrific support system. Rather than shame his son for having sexual thoughts, he shows Jim various porn magazines and gives him advice on how to talk to girls. The scenes between Jim and his dad are uncomfortable in a touching and funny way because it's obvious that Mr. Levenstein wants to be seen as hip and cool. He also cares deeply about his son and doesn't want him feeling awkward or isolated.

Chris Ostreicher, known as "Oz" to his friends, is a star lacrosse player. He envisions himself as a modern-day Casanova. He joins the school jazz choir because he believes showing a sensitive side will help him win girls and show himself as more than just a jock. Justifying his actions, he tells his friends that talking to girls is easy because all he needs to do is simply ask them some questions and then listen to whatever they have to say. Oz's narrow-minded attitude, which is shared by many of the male characters in the film, is immature and naïve, as well as misogynistic.

Finally, there is Steve Stifler, who is popular and athletic, wanting to be the center of attention. He swears constantly and makes fun of people because he is narcissistic. He enjoys asserting his superiority. He throws wild parties and flirts with girls because he is interested in them as conquests instead of as friends. Though he is crude and unlikable, Stifler is one of the film's funniest characters because he is also one of the most unpredictable. We never know what he is going to say or when he is going to say it.

American Pie succeeds in capturing the nervousness associated with being sexually inexperienced and with the social stigma created by not having engaged in adult activities. The characters are so concerned with having sex that they run the risk of not enjoying their senior year to the fullest. At one point, Jim tells his friends, "You realize we're all going to go to college as virgins. They probably have special dorms for people like us." The five friends need to learn how to communicate properly, not only with girls but with each other.

These five young men believe that being caring and sensitive are negative qualities, but what they don't understand is that it's precisely their lack of those important qualities that keeps them from enjoying positive and nurturing relationships with the opposite sex. Though the film is often vulgar in its dialogue and actions, it is also sweet and comical in its presentation of friendship and the need to be accepted.

Why You Should See This Film: Because, like an apple pie, it's both tart and sweet, celebrating a raunchy series of adventures involving a close group of friends.

Main Themes: Deception * Selfishness * Peer Pressure * Insecurity * Friendship

Classic Line: "I would like to make an announcement. There is a gorgeous woman masturbating on my bed."

Recommended Double Feature: *The Sure Thing* (1985); Rated PG-13, 100 minutes, Comedy-drama-romance

THE BABYSITTER
(2017)

Directed by: McG
Written by: Brian Duffield
Cast: Judah Lewis (Cole), Samara Weaving (Bee), Emily Alyn Lind (Melanie), Leslie Bibb (Mom), Ken Marino (Dad)
Rating: Rated TV-MA for profanity, sexual language, extreme violence, and gore
Runtime: 85 minutes
Genre: Horror-comedy

The Gist: Equally hilarious and shocking, this is a coming-of-age story disguised as a horror film. Cole is a twelve-year-old who's on the wrong side of adolescence. He acts more like a skittish child than a budding teenager. Several scenes at the beginning of the film illustrate his fear and trepidation: he is scared of receiving a shot in the arm while sitting in the nurse's office, a basketball is thrown at his head twice, and three bullies taunt and tease him on his way home from school.

Cole doesn't have many friends. He doesn't stand up for himself and he's afraid to take chances. He needs to beef up his self-confidence, and later in the film he's forced to do so in order to stay alive. An introvert, Cole only has two friends. One is Melanie, a neighbor who is Cole's age. She and Cole clearly like each other, though Cole is too nervous to act on his feelings. The other friend is Bee, who is Cole's gorgeous babysitter. Early in the film, while Cole is being bullied by three boys, it's Bee who comes to his rescue. She whispers menacing words and then pops a tire on one of their bikes.

However, Cole is not naïve. He understands his limitations. After his encounter with the three bullies, Bee drives him home in her cool car, and we see the roof of his treehouse lying in a heap on the side of the road. Cole tells Bee they are taking it down and then he remarks that treehouses are just for kids. He realizes he's approaching an age where he needs to start thinking more about cars and girls and less about toys and playing in a treehouse. This is more apparent after Bee drops him off at home. Cole stares at her breasts with a dazed look on his face, and then he compliments her jeep, asking if she still plans to give it to him.

Cole's parents don't have much screen time, but they are loving and supportive. His father takes Cole to a deserted parking lot and tries to teach him how to drive, but Cole is too scared and just sits there with his hands on the steering wheel. Later, he asks his mother if she thinks he's a wimp. He feels inadequate for being afraid of everything. Rather than yell at him, his mother looks at him with affection and says, "You are at a time in your life where a lot of things are scary. But as you get older, those same things will stop frightening you as much." Her advice is poignant in that it acknowledges the changes he is going through, both physically and emotionally. At the same time, her words foreshadow the gruesome events still to come.

The film revs into high gear once Cole's parents leave for a trip. Bee arrives to babysit, and there is a sweet montage of the two characters bonding. They perform silly dance moves, swim in the pool, watch *Billy Jack* on an outdoor movie screen, cook pizza, and discuss which famous characters they would select for an intergalactic dream team on a mission. It's clear during these moments that Cole has a crush on Bee. He admires her not just because she is beautiful, but because she is older and hip. She's a confident young woman who doesn't take shit from anyone.

After talking with Melanie—who tells Cole that babysitters have sex with their boyfriends after their charges go to bed—he decides to stay up so he can find out what usually happens after he typically falls asleep. Eventually, he hears a group of people enter the house, and when he sneaks halfway down the stairs to spy on them, he discovers Bee and her high school friends playing a game of spin the bottle. However, the innocent game soon turns deadly.

The rest of the film deals with Cole trying to evade a bunch of would-be killers. There are plenty of inventive kills, and copious amounts of blood are splattered across the screen. There are also several witty one-liners and humorous moments. To stay alive, Cole must find the courage to combat his fears, and the film is clever in how it mirrors scenes from the first half of the film—in which he was scared and hesitant—with scenes from the second half of the film that present similar situations, but now showcase Cole's growth and newfound daringness, such as a heartfelt conversation with Melanie or his determination to crash a car into his house with the radio blaring.

Chock full of clever dialogue, *The Babysitter* shows the darker side of maturity. By depicting Cole's transition from childhood to adolescence through the lens of a violent horror story, the film demonstrates how traumatic and stressful these crucial moments in life can sometimes be. It also reveals how we sometimes remain passive until we find ourselves in the midst of painful and intimidating moments that force us to be dynamic and productive in both our actions and our decisions. That these experiences are vital to our maturity is emphasized at the end of the film when Cole tells his parents, in a strong and commanding voice, that he doesn't need a babysitter anymore.

Why You Should See This Film: Because it's a search for independence and self-identity wrapped up in a blood-soaked night of terror.

Main Themes: Survival * Courage * Bullying * Self-Awareness * Innocence

Classic Line: "Things get messy when you make a deal with the devil."

Recommended Double Feature: *Jennifer's Body* (2009); Rated R, 107 minutes, Horror

BETTER OFF DEAD
(1985)

Directed by: Savage Steve Holland
Written by: Savage Steve Holland
Cast: John Cusack (Lane), David Ogden Stiers (Al), Kim Darby (Jenny), Diane Franklin (Monique), Dan Schneider (Ricky), Amanda Wyss (Beth), Curtis Armstrong (Charles)
Rating: Rated PG for adult situations and adult language
Runtime: 97 minutes
Genre: Comedy

The Gist: Anyone who has ever been dumped can relate to Lane Myer. He's a high school student who lives for two things: skiing and his girlfriend, Beth. Lane is completely obsessed with her. They've been dating for six months, and pictures of Beth are plastered on every square inch of wall space in his bedroom. Clearly, this is not a healthy relationship. Everything Lane says and does is meant to impress his girlfriend, including the purchase of a Camaro that he doesn't drive because it rests under a tarp in his front yard.

The opening credits hint at the film's themes and conflicts. A cartoon shows a green monster carrying away a screaming blonde. They rush past a knight, who instantly falls in love with the maiden. He proceeds to rescue her but gives up when the monster jumps over a ravine. Together, the knight and his horse jump into a river filled with alligators. Besides love and the idea of pursuit, these opening credits point to the importance of doubt and uncertainty in the film, namely, Lane's lack of confidence.

When Lane wakes up in the morning, he promptly pulls a framed picture of Beth from under the covers. He gazes at it, kisses it, and then he takes the picture into the bathroom while he showers. His behavior might seem eccentric to most people, but Lane's entire household is extremely quirky. His mother is a terrible cook and serves the most disgusting food, some of which actually crawls off the plate. His father is in a fight with the paperboy, who keeps smashing the garage windows whenever he rides by on his bike and hurls the newspaper. Then there's his younger brother, Badger, a quiet kid who mails in cereal coupons for random prizes like a book titled *How to Pick Up Trashy Women*.

Lane decides to try out for the high school ski team, but he doesn't make the cut. On the ride home, Beth breaks up with him, announcing she needs to go out with someone who is more popular and who drives a nicer car. Worse, she leaves him for the captain of the ski team, who's an arrogant jerk, but is good looking and popular. More importantly, he's the only person in their hometown of Greendale, California, who has skied the K12 from the glacier and survived.

Distraught over the breakup, Lane decides to kill himself. While suicide is a serious issues, his numerous failed attempts are presented as more humorous than somber, and they do elicit laughs. For instance, he tries to hang himself in the garage, but then realizes he hasn't been anywhere yet. As he is about to remove the noose, his mom opens the door to vacuum and knocks him off the step. The film is not downplaying the severity of suicide, but exaggerating the obsession Lane has toward Beth. In doing so, it illustrates the disconnect between Lane and the rest of his family, suggesting that perhaps if he had someone close to talk with about his relationship, then perhaps he could better process his emotions.

In addition to Lane's weird family, there are an assortment of odd characters in the film who provide plenty of laughs. There is the infamous paperboy who yells, "I want my two dollars!" throughout the film as he stalks Lane to collect his fee. There is also Lane's close friend Charles De Mar who laments that he can't score real drugs in Greendale, so he snorts random substances like pure snow and Jell-O. Then there is Ricky, a neighbor and fellow student who rarely speaks. Ricky lives with his mother, snorts too much nasal spray, and excels at slurping up Jell-O with a straw in the school cafeteria. While these characters are certainly strange in their dialogue and mannerisms, many of them are exaggerations of the various cliques found in most high schools.

Spending the year with Ricky and his mom is Monique. She's a foreign exchange student from France. Monique is a pretty girl who hates living with Ricky because he is creepy and treats her like his girlfriend. She much prefers to spend time with Lane. She boosts his self-esteem, convincing him to stand up for himself. She says, "I think all you need is a small taste of success, and you will find it suits you." Still upset over his breakup with Beth, Lane gravitates toward Monique. They form a friendship that becomes the healthiest relationship in the film.

It's sometimes hard to empathize with Lane because he's apathetic and can't envision a world without Beth. What he needs to do is just quit sulking. He needs to understand that it's more important to be with someone who enjoys him for who he is rather than someone who judges him for what he's not. And he needs to be more active in bettering his own life. To his credit, he does take this crucial step when he challenges the ski captain to a race on the infamous K12. The deadly mountain represents a physical and emotional test for Lane. But with a zany cast of characters surrounding him, forcing him to be more dynamic and assertive, he might just realize he's not as much of a victim as he makes himself out to be.

Why You Should See This Film: Because it's a hilarious cult classic about teen crushes and dealing with rejection.

Main Themes: Communication * Self-Confidence * Disillusionment * Love * Perseverance

Classic Line: "Gee, I'm really sorry your mom blew up, Ricky. The doctor says she'll be okay, I guess, but she won't be able to eat any spicy foods for a while."

Recommended Double Feature: *One Crazy Summer* (1986); Rated PG, 93 minutes, Comedy

BILLY ELLIOT
(2000)

Directed by: Stephen Daldry
Written by: Lee Hall
Cast: Jamie Bell (Billy), Julie Walters (Mrs. Wilkinson), Stuart Wells (Michael), Gary Lewis (Jackie), Jean Heywood (Grandma), Jamie Draven (Tony)
Rating: Rated R for strong language
Runtime: 110 minutes
Genre: Drama-comedy

The Gist: This British film is about following one's dreams in the face of adversity. That it's a coming-of-age film makes it even more. The title character, Billy Elliot, is an eleven-year-old boy who lives in county Durham in North East England. The year is 1984. Billy lives in a lower-class neighborhood with his father (Jackie), his older brother (Tony), and his grandmother who has Alzheimer's disease. His mother has died, and it's clear his father is struggling to raise two children. To complicate matters, Billy's father and brother used to work in the coal mine, but they are now on strike, which only adds to the family's hardships.

Billy loves music. He listens to his brother's records, and oftentimes he will break into dance moves while walking down the street. As the opening credits flash across the screen, Billy puts on a record and jumps up and down on his bed. He dances as he prepares breakfast in the kitchen, constantly moving in rhythm to the music. These opening scenes are important because they illustrate Billy's cramped living conditions and dreary surroundings. They also introduce his affection for music and dance, both of which help him escape from the anger and loneliness surrounding his drab home life.

Afternoons, Billy goes to the boy's club to box. However, he's neither very good nor interested. When he puts on the gloves and tries to box, he dances awkwardly around the ring. His coach tells Billy how terrible he is, and that he disgraces the boxing gloves. Sentenced to serve time at a punching bag that's almost as big as he is, Billy swings several uncoordinated punches. He then watches the bag swing left and right, moving rhythmically to the tune of the ballet music that is drifting over from the other side of the hall.

Because of the coal miners' strike, the ballet class must use part of the hall. Billy becomes more interested in what the ballet class is doing than in what the boxing class is doing. Gradually, he moves over to the other side of the room to watch the ballet dancers, entranced by their fluidity and movement. Billy joins in for the rest of the class, but when the ballet teacher (Mrs. Wilkinson) asks him if he plans to continue, he appears hesitant. He tells her he feels like a sissy. It's clear that Billy enjoys ballet,

Jamie Bell, Gary Lewis. ***USA Films/Photofest © USA Films***

but he also knows that boxing is considered a man's activity while ballet is considered a woman's activity.

Thus begins Billy Elliot's secret life in which he pretends to attend boxing classes, but secretly practices ballet. He has a true gift for dancing and loves it. He hides the ballet shoes under his bed and steals a ballet book from the library so he can practice his form at home. Whether he is alone in his bedroom or brushing his teeth in the bathroom, he rehearses various dance moves and pirouettes. He's frustrated when he falls or topples over, but he remains steadfast in his determination to become a skilled performer. Billy's confidence grows as he becomes stronger and more graceful. When he finally accomplishes his first pirouette, he is ecstatic and runs through the streets as if he has just conquered the world.

His father, however, doesn't support Billy's interest in ballet. He tells his son that men should play football or wrestle. The only person Billy can confide in is his friend, Michael, who is gay and understands all too well what it feels like to be in the minority. As the film progresses, Billy shifts from caring more about what other people think to making his own decisions and standing up for his own opinions. Rather than passively watch his life unfold, he becomes active in steering it down a desired path.

The awkward situation intensifies even more when Mrs. Wilkinson wants Billy to audition for the Royal Ballet School. She becomes a mother figure who encourages him to ignore the taunts and jeers. She helps him to be proud of his talents. Billy himself, once hesitant about becoming a ballet dancer, now feels invigorated by his newfound passion, and announces to his father that lots of men are ballet dancers.

Eventually, Billy's family realizes that attending the Royal Ballet School is an opportunity for him to escape the stifling conditions of the coal mining community. But there is little money to pay for the trip to London or for the audition. Billy's father, who supports the miners and their strike, must decide whether or not to cross the picket lines and work. He wants to be loyal to his friends and fight for a cause he believes in, but he also wants to give his children a chance to achieve their dreams.

There is chaos everywhere in Billy Elliot's life. The miners are striking, his family is battling financial hardships and trying to process his mother's death, and Billy is struggling to be happy with ballet despite the expectations of others. Yes, the film is dramatic and moving, but it is also funny and enthusiastic. It presents a group of characters who truly care about each other, even if they don't always know how to show it.

Why You Should See This Film: Because it's a celebration of individuality in which personal ambition conflicts with societal expectations.
Main Themes: Prejudice * Class * Perseverance * Family * Responsibility
Classic Line: "I don't want a childhood. I want to be a ballet dancer."
Recommended Double Feature: *Don't Talk to Irene* (2017); Rated TV-14, 90 minutes, Comedy

THE BREADWINNER
(2017)

Directed by: Nora Twomey
Written by: Anita Doron, based on the novel by Deborah Ellis
Cast: Saara Chaudry (Parvana), Soma Chhaya (Shauzia), Ali Badshah (Nurullah), Laara Sadiq (Fattema), Kawa Ada (Razaq)
Rating: Rated PG-13 for thematic material including some violent images
Runtime: 94 minutes
Genre: Drama-animation

The Gist: This animated film takes place in Kabul, Afghanistan, and focuses on an eleven-year-old girl named Parvana who lives with her family under the oppressive rule of the Taliban. Her father, Nurullah, is a former teacher. He is disabled as a result of fighting in a war. He has one leg and walks with a large cane. Each day, he sits with Parvana in the marketplace and the two of them attempt to sell various family items so they can earn enough money to eat.

When the film opens, Parvana's father is arrested. He has been targeted by a former student who joined the Taliban. This young man believes he was insulted in the marketplace after arguing with Parvana's father. Since there is no male figure in the household, Parvana must work hard to ensure her family's survival. They live in a small apartment and must go outside each day to fetch water from a well. But women are not allowed to be seen in public unless they are accompanied by a man, so

Parvana (voiced by Saara Chaudry). ***Universal Pictures/Photofest © Universal Pictures***

Parvana must disguise herself as a boy. Her concealment is dangerous, for if it's discovered she is a girl, then she could be thrown in jail or killed.

The numerous hardships Parvana endures throughout the film speak as much to the trials of becoming independent and of learning personal responsibility as they do to the tyrannical presence of the Taliban. For example, she tries to persuade her mother (Fattema) not to visit the jail, but her mother insists and is beaten. Parvana then has to escort her mother home and tend to her wounds. During these scenes, we see Parvana assume the parent role. She cuts her hair and braves her way into the marketplace, standing tall and speaking with confidence. During these moments, she finally understands what it means to be seen and heard in a patriarchal society.

It's clear from the opening scenes that women are viewed as inferior to men. Any woman seen by herself outside of the home is immediately attacked, either verbally or physically. For example, Parvana is nervous simply fetching water from the well in the middle of the day. As well, no one in the marketplace will talk to Parvana or sell her food while she is a girl wandering around without a male chaperone. But as soon as she disguises herself as a boy, the shopkeepers joke with her and treat her like a respectable customer.

Parvana soon meets another girl named Shauzia who has also disguised herself as a boy. Shauzia wants to save enough money so she can escape to the coast and finally see the ocean. For her, the vastness of the water represents freedom and an opportunity to run away from her father. Together, the two girls work odd jobs, scraping together money however and whenever they can. Parvana also befriends a man named Razaq whom she teaches to read and write. These few scenes with Razaq illustrate how the horrors of war extend to men and women of all ages, and they show the importance of empathy.

Parvana is surrounded by death and danger on a daily basis, and it has forced her to grow up faster than she should. While Parvana's story might seem like a fantasy to some viewers, the tragic truth is that many young adults who live under these oppressive conditions must assume adult responsibilities if they wish to stay alive. At home, Parvana's mother tells her, "Don't be in such a hurry to grow up. It might not be all that you expect." And Parvana's father, before his arrest, confesses that he wants her to remain a child. He seems to understand how their daily hardships—many of which stem from a country wracked by invasions and a civil war—have stripped away her innocence and the playfulness she should be exhibiting as a young girl.

The colors in the film tend to be mostly browns and blacks and grays, all somber shades that add to the depressing atmosphere in which Parvana and her family live. Many of the characters are dressed in similar colors, stressing the conformity to which everyone is expected to adhere in a Taliban-ruled society. In contrast, Parvana and her family are shown wearing vivid colors like blue and red and green. These bright colors allude to the love and connectedness shared by the family, and they suggest there is always hope in a world that often appears so difficult and unfair.

Later in the film, Parvana uses her newfound conviction to visit the jail all by herself, hoping to bribe one of the guards with money so she can see her father. Her desire to reunite her family is represented by the name she chooses for herself when she is disguised as a boy: Aatish. It means "fire," and in naming herself, Parvana gives herself a power and strength she has never known. As Aatish, she learns to be a provider, and it affords her confidence to embark on her perilous journey.

The end of the film is a wonderful mix of suspense and action and redemption. Parvana struggles to find her father as the war closes in. In doing so, she demonstrates patience and intelligence while avoiding the Taliban and refusing to surrender. She must rely on family and friendships to supply her with hope. And she must face her own fears while exploring new and dangerous landscapes.

Why You Should See This Film: Because it's a sobering account of a family's fight for survival amid oppression and injustice.

Main Themes: War * Survival * Family * Courage * Power

Classic Line: "Raise your words, not your voice. It is rain that grows flowers, not thunder."

Recommended Double Feature: *Persepolis* (2007); Rated PG-13, 96 minutes, Drama-animation

THE BREAKFAST CLUB
(1985)

Directed by: John Hughes
Written by: John Hughes
Cast: Molly Ringwald (Claire), Emilio Estevez (Andrew), Anthony Michael Hall (Brian), Ally Sheedy (Allison), Judd Nelson (Bender), Paul Gleason (Principal Vernon)
Rating: Rated R for adult content and adult language
Runtime: 97 minutes
Genre: Comedy-drama

The Gist: One of the most popular coming-of-age films ever made, *The Breakfast Club* endures because it speaks to any generation. Being a teenager has always been difficult. There are conflicts with parents and friends, and there are struggles with career choices and academic expectations. But *The Breakfast Club* explores these difficulties by placing five very different students in a high school library for eight hours and letting their emotions simmer until the tension explodes in a series of honest and poignant conversations. It's not afraid to show that, sometimes, high school can be a hot mess.

Over the course of one day, the five main characters—Andrew, Brian, Claire, Bender, and Allison—try to understand themselves and each other. They express anger toward their own parents, and they're upset at being trapped within a particular label. Indeed, each of them represents a well-known clique that wanders the hallways of almost every high school:

a brain, an athlete, a basket case, a princess, and a criminal. The idea of fitting in is stressed at the beginning of the film when Claire tells Principal Vernon that she doesn't think she belongs in the room with everyone else. These five students only socialize with their respective peer groups. They're unsure how to approach each other in such a small setting. And while it's clear that each of them resents the others and looks down upon them, they do so because they're judging them based solely on preconceived definitions of a specific clique.

While *The Breakfast Club* is often funny, there are several intense and awkward scenes. Throughout the film, Principal Vernon verbally attacks Bender in a way that would definitely get him fired today. He even challenges the student to a fistfight. Other times, Claire calls Allison a bitch and Brian tells Claire she's conceited. In an especially powerful scene, Andrew yells at Bender, "You don't even count. If you disappeared forever it wouldn't make any difference. You may as well not even exist at this school." Andrew's words resonate because the opposite of love is apathy, not hatred. At some point in our lives we've all been bullied or ignored. We understand how these characters feel when they're attacked by their peers. We also understand that not being recognized can make us feel useless and insignificant.

Emilio Estevez, Anthony Michael Hall. ***Universal Pictures/Photofest © Universal Pictures***

There are several homophobic slurs uttered throughout the film, and the characters discuss topics like depression, suicide, and sex. Sometimes they discuss these topics in a friendly manner, other times in a heated debate that reveals their personal fears and prejudices. For example, Allison claims to be a nymphomaniac, then admits she's a compulsive liar. And Bender is resentful of Claire's money and Brian's grade point average. Upon noticing Claire's diamond earrings, Bender remarks that for Christmas he received a carton of cigarettes from his abusive father.

During the film, Bender bullies the others, especially Claire. In one scene, while he is hiding underneath a table, he stares at Claire's crotch. Transfixed, he moves forward for a closer look at her underwear until she realizes his head is between her legs. Immediately following this scene—after Claire has expressed her disgust by slapping him—she is first to leave the group so she can join him to smoke a joint. While these scenes and confrontations address issues of gender and power, they also reveal five characters who are not as smart and savvy as they think they are. They're confused and frustrated, victims of societal and peer expectations.

And though Bender is the troublemaker, his defiance and bad-boy image represent a freedom and uncaringness that the others wish they possessed. Like most teenagers, they crave independence. They believe their parents don't understand them. More importantly, they believe their parents don't try to understand them. Watching these characters interact—listening to them talk about their problems at home and at school—it's apparent that what they really want is to be taken seriously. They want to be inspired and encouraged. But at home they feel pressured to meet their parents' expectations while at school they struggle to either fit in with their friends or avoid confrontations with other peer groups.

Adolescents know they can always surround themselves with like-minded people who understand them. However, being in a clique separates them from others by labeling them as different. The attraction of *The Breakfast Club* is that we can all relate to these five characters. There are bits and pieces of them inside each one of us, pulsing with confusion and hope and defiance. Those parts—however whole or fractured they might be—are important traits that help to define our own identities, whether we're a brain, an athlete, a basket case, a princess, or a criminal.

Why You Should See This Film: Because it's a vivid display of anger and resentment morphing into heartfelt honesty during a Saturday detention.

Main Themes: Bullying * Peer Pressure * Individuality * Empowerment * Rebelliousness

Classic Line: "We're all pretty bizarre. Some of us are just better at hiding it, that's all."

Recommended Double Feature: *Weird Science* (1985); Rated PG-13, 94 minutes, Comedy-fantasy

CALL ME BY YOUR NAME (2017)

Directed by: Luca Guadagnino
Written by: James Ivory, based on the novel by Andre Aciman
Cast: Timothée Chalamet (Elio), Armie Hammer (Oliver), Michael Stuhlbarg (Mr. Perlman), Amira Casar (Mrs. Perlman), Esther Garrel (Marzia)
Rating: Rated R for adult content, adult language, mild violence, nudity, and strong sexual content
Runtime: 132 minutes
Genre: Drama-romance

The Gist: This beautiful and affecting love story takes place during the summer of 1983 in northern Italy. Elio is seventeen years old. An avid reader and a talented musician, he is quiet and keeps to himself. At home, he reads novels, transcribes music, and plays the piano. He bikes around the village and traipses through the lush countryside. Sometimes, he swims in the river and picks fresh fruit off the trees. He has no cares or worries, and his summer vacation can best be described as tranquil.

Elio's father (Mr. Perlman) is an archeology professor. As the film begins a twenty-four-year-old graduate student named Oliver arrives for a six-week stay. He has been chosen to help Elio's father organize his academic papers and to catalog his slides. Oliver is intelligent and good looking, as extroverted as Elio is introverted. At first, Elio dislikes Oliver. He finds him impolite and arrogant. He is upset that he must give up his bedroom during Oliver's stay. And he tells his parents that he doesn't like the way Oliver says, "Later" upon leaving the dinner table. Elio seems jealous of the way their new visitor can command attention and make friends. He admires Oliver's carefree attitude.

But then Elio shows Oliver around town. They bike and swim together. They talk about music. Elio pays more attention to what Oliver says and does, and he finds himself attracted to the older man. He becomes jealous when he sees Oliver making out with a woman on the dance floor during a party. So Elio begins a sexual relationship with a girl named Marzia. She adores him, but he seems disinterested. Then, at breakfast one morning, Elio tells his father he almost had sex with Marzia. When his father asks him why he didn't, Elio admits he didn't have the courage.

This is a story about understanding those first pangs of lust and attraction. It's about two people discovering each other and sharing a part of themselves. Elio brags about Marzia because he wants to make Oliver jealous. But it's also clear that spending time with the graduate student has inspired Elio to be more assertive. He is inexperienced when it comes to love, and he struggles with how, or even when, to tell Oliver about his intimate feelings.

One afternoon, while Elio and his parents are sitting on the couch, Elio's mother reads aloud a passage from a sixteenth-century French romance novel. It's about a knight and a princess. After his mother finishes reading, she asks them whether it is better to speak or to die. Elio's parents suspect he and Oliver share more than a friendship, and the subtext of their conversation centers around the difficulty in expressing one's true feelings because there is always the possibility of rejection.

Elio's dad takes him and Oliver to Lake Garda where an archeological treasure has been brought up from the water. It's part of a famous statue that sunk centuries ago during a shipwreck. As the rest of the statue is raised from the bottom of the ocean, there is an overwhelming sense of wonder and excitement. There is also a strong connection between this historical find and the developing relationship between Elio and Oliver. In both instances, romantic feelings are being brought to the surface.

Call Me by Your Name is an intimate film. It has a slow, deliberate rhythm. The lazy summer days create a peaceful serenity that allows the characters to think and reflect. They lie in the grass and stare up at the sky. They flirt openly, but with hesitation. There is an innocent playfulness in the way Elio and Oliver finally succumb to their desires. The scenes between them are tender and passionate. They are not explicit in their sexuality, but heartfelt in their truthfulness.

Oliver says he doesn't want Elio to regret anything. He is old enough to know that their special relationship is temporary. Elio, however, struggles with the fact that Oliver's time in Italy is coming to an end. He doesn't know how to deal with their impending separation. He has so many new feelings to express, but he doesn't always know how to convey them properly.

During this time, Elio's parents remain loving and supportive. At the end of the film, he and his father sit down for an emotional conversation about love and heartache. Mr. Perlman tells Elio that we should never try to make ourselves feel nothing, and that we should use the pain and sorrow we suffer to make us feel more alive. He says, "We rip out so much of ourselves to be cured of things faster than we should that we go bankrupt by the age of thirty and have less to offer each time we start with someone new." It's a brilliant and beautiful monologue that is more than just a concerned father offering his son important advice. It's also a poignant reminder of how every one of us should approach our own passions and responsibilities.

Why You Should See This Film: Because it's a deeply moving story about the joys and pains of first love during an idyllic summer.

Main Themes: Courage * Sexual Discovery * Honesty * Communication * Grief

Classic Line: "If you only knew how little I know about the things that matter."

Recommended Double Feature: *Y Tu Mama Tambien* (2001); Rated R, 106 minutes, Drama-comedy

CHRISTINE
(1983)

Directed by: John Carpenter
Written by: Bill Phillips, based on the novel by Stephen King
Cast: Keith Gordon (Arnie), John Stockwell (Dennis), Alexandra Paul (Leigh)
Rating: Rated R for strong language and violence
Runtime: 110 minutes
Genre: Horror

The Gist: A film about a possessed car might seem like an odd choice as essential viewing for teenagers. But while most coming-of-age films show the growth of a main character, *Christine* shows how adolescent development can be impeded by obsession and jealousy. The film also shows how isolating oneself from friends and parents can create angry and violent situations. The main character's love for his car symbolizes an unhealthy high school relationship built upon need and dependency. In fact, the film succeeds as a coming-of-age story precisely because it reveals how bad decisions can be detrimental to one's maturity.

Arnie Cunningham is a nerdy and unpopular kid who wears glasses and dresses like a slob. His best friend is Dennis, a player on the football team. Dennis protects Arnie from bullies at school, but his home life isn't much better. His parents treat him like a child. They never allow him the opportunity to express his own opinions and always assume they know exactly what he needs. Arnie conforms to everyone around him. As a result, his maturity has been stunted.

One day, on their way home from school, Arnie spots a 1958 red Plymouth Fury for sale and falls instantly in love with it. The car's name is Christine, and unbeknownst to Arnie the car has a shady past that involves several people dying in it. Despite the car looking like it's ready for the junkyard, Arnie purchases it. When Dennis asks him why he likes Christine so much, Arnie tells him, "Maybe it's just that for the first time in my life I found something that's uglier than me." Clearly, Arnie has self-esteem issues, but he is also a victim of love at first sight, and this impulsivity sets in motion the dark and tragic events that occur throughout the rest of the film.

As Arnie fixes up the car, he undergoes a transformation himself. He begins dating a beautiful girl named Leigh. He dresses like a 1950s teenager and becomes more arrogant and confrontational, especially when interacting with his parents. He also shuns Dennis, choosing to spend all of his time repairing Christine and fixating on his new possession. Certainly, the word "possession" implies that an evil spirit resides inside the car, but it also alludes to the obsessive way that Arnie treasures his new car.

Eventually, Arnie becomes more distant from his friends and family. He wears red shirts and jackets, which symbolize his intimate bond with Christine. The color red suggests lust and anger, two emotions evident in Arnie's transformation throughout the film. The fact that Christine is a Plymouth Fury—the word "fury" characterizing the car itself as passionate and malicious—foreshadows the control she will wield over Arnie. Once restored, the car makes her first appearance at a high school football game. In a classic image, Arnie kisses Leigh while leaning against his car, and this shot sets up a creepy love triangle. Feeling confidant, Arnie is showing off both his girl and his car, considering them both as his treasured possessions. That he prizes his own car above his girlfriend, however, shows how people often use material objects to define themselves. However, those same material objects can sometimes turn them into selfish and conceited jerks.

During the film, several people die, either those who wrong Arnie and Christine or those who attempt to come between them. Just like Leigh is jealous of Arnie's infatuation with Christine, it seems Christine is also jealous of Arnie's affection for Leigh. Clearly, the importance of peer and family relationships, and how we juggle those relationships, is a key lesson in the film. As the killings continue, Arnie becomes less of a person and more of an object, a symbol of wrath and isolation trapped behind a steering wheel.

Christine dominates Arnie, but she also affords him a sense of control that he's never possessed before, not just in dating Leigh but in standing up to his parents. There are physical and emotional struggles at home as Arnie becomes more outspoken and combative. Arnie believes his parents treat him like a child because they don't want him to grow up. He tells Dennis that his parents act the way they do because they are afraid of growing old. While this attitude illustrates Arnie's anger and resentment—which is fueled by his new look and hip attitude—it also touches on the power shift that occurs between adolescents and their parents. It's true that Arnie's parents are overbearing, and perhaps if the three of them had communicated more effectively, then Arnie might not have rebelled so violently.

It's easy to understand the lure of Christine. She is basically a sex object. She looks cool and warrants second glances from passersby. Toward the end of the film, while speeding down the road, Arnie declares that there is nothing better than driving his own car. After so many years of being bullied and ridiculed, he loves the attention and authority that Christine provides for him. Sure, it's fun to have a status symbol you can show off to your friends, but not when it constantly runs people over.

Why You Should See This Film: Because it's a gripping search for independence that leads to a scary descent into madness.

Main Themes: Jealousy * Obsession * Anger * Bullying * Fear

Classic Line: "Has it ever occurred to you that part of being a parent is trying to kill your kids?"

Recommended Double Feature: *Carrie* (1976); Rated R, 98 minutes, Horror-drama

CLUELESS
(1995)

Directed by: Amy Heckerling
Written by: Amy Heckerling
Cast: Alicia Silverstone (Cher), Stacey Dash (Dionne), Brittany Murphy (Tai), Paul Rudd (Josh), Dan Hedaya (Mel)
Rating: Rated PG-13 for adult content, adult language, and mild violence
Runtime: 100 minutes
Genre: Comedy

The Gist: Loosely based on Jane Austen's classic 1815 novel *Emma*, the story focuses on a girl named Cher as she navigates life at her posh high school. Cher is beautiful, popular, and spoiled. She uses a computer program to select her outfit each day, and all of the clothes in her closet rotate on an electronic carousel. In fact, she's so concerned with her appearance that when she's mugged late at night she is more concerned with ruining her dress than with the gun the man is holding. Everything in Cher's life, from her friends to her accessories, is a status symbol that accentuates her wealth and attractiveness.

Cher lives in a mansion with her father, Mel. He's a powerful litigator who is always working on a court case. He is extremely protective of his only child and dotes on her with a combination of gruffness and sweetness. He lectures her on grades and is critical of her clothing, telling her at one point that the dress she's wearing looks like underwear. But he grudgingly accepts her constant attempts to make him eat healthy. And when

Alicia Silverstone, Brittany Murphy, Stacey Dash. ***Paramount Pictures/Photofest © Paramount Pictures***

she argues her way to better grades on her report card, he is impressed with her negotiating skills. Though he is demanding and overprotective, he is also extremely proud of his daughter.

Cher hangs out with a tight group of friends. There's her best friend Dionne and Dionne's boyfriend Murray. Then there's Tai, an awkward and homely girl whom Cher considers a project, which means she takes Tai shopping and teaches her how to behave. In this way, Cher resembles Jane Austen's character Emma, someone who enjoys matchmaking and meddling in other people's lives. Though Cher is not the most intelligent person, she does have a big heart. For example, she decides to set up two of her teachers because she thinks they look cute together. Later, she tries to set up Tai with a popular, good-looking boy.

Despite seeming like an airhead, Cher has moments where she shows us she is not just a ditzy girl in designer jeans. In fact, it's her bubbly personality and generosity that make her so likable and funny. When a literary snob tries to argue with Cher that Hamlet said, "To thine own self be true," Cher corrects her by quoting Mel Gibson's version of Hamlet. She is also honest, admitting that she is a virgin when everyone around her is talking about sex. And her desire to befriend Tai, rather than make fun of her appearance and the way she talks, suggests she is warm and caring. These moments illustrate Cher's self-confidence and help to humanize her because we see she is not as shallow and self-absorbed as many of her friends.

The film embodies the nineties generation and attitude of high school students. Cher and her friends speak in hip nineties slang. They say catchy phrases like, "Oh my God, I am totally buggin'" and "She's a full-on Monet. From far away, it's okay. But up close, it's a big old mess." The film's clever slang, along with the characters' social status, present a world and lifestyle that might seem like a fantasy to contemporary viewers. For instance, Cher remarks that her house is classic because the columns date back to 1972.

Clueless focuses not just on Cher's relationship with her friends, but also on the relationship she has with her stepbrother, Josh. They constantly bicker with each other whenever he visits the house, though in an amusing way rather than in a mean-spirited way. Cher criticizes his serious attitude and his attempts to be more adultlike in the way he talks. Josh makes fun of her immature mannerisms and her lack of knowledge on world events and issues. He is genuinely amazed during one scene when Cher watches the news as if studying for an exam. The developing relationship between Cher and Josh is a crucial part of her self-discovery. She begins to realize that instead of always trying to help others and make them happy, she needs to focus more on her own happiness.

The film highlights the emotional and academic ignorance of rich, preppy students who are given so many accessories and privileges that they have no concept of personal responsibility. Most of them lack a personal identity because their self-identity is based on their shallow interpretations of how their friends perceive them. Toward the end of the film, Cher laments that everything she says and does is wrong. This is an important moment of self-revelation because she understands that her seemingly perfect life is complicated and in need of repair. Like her friends, Cher has been clueless. All of them are so immersed in their own material world that they can't even drive on the L.A. freeway without believing they're going to die. They feel safe and secure inside their own expensive bubbles where everything they know, and everything they do, is convenient and self-serving. At some point, though—whether we like it or not—we all need to get on that freeway so we can drive away to explore our surroundings.

Why You Should See This Film: Because it's a funny and satirical look at glitzy teen life in Beverly Hills.

Main Themes: Pretentiousness * Naïveté * Obsession * Selfishness * Apathy

Classic Line: "Anything happens to my daughter, I got a .45 and a shovel. I doubt anybody would miss you."

Recommended Double Feature: *10 Things I Hate about You* (1999); Rated PG-13, 99 minutes, Romantic comedy

COMING THROUGH THE RYE

(2015)

Directed by: James Steven Sadwith
Written by: James Steven Sadwith
Cast: Chris Cooper (J. D. Salinger), Alex Wolff (Jamie), Stefania LaVie Owen (Deedee), Zephyr Benson (Gerry)
Rating: Rated PG-13 for some drug material, sexuality, and language
Runtime: 97 minutes
Genre: Drama

The Gist: Inspired by real events, the story takes place in 1969 and focuses on Jamie Schwartz, a sixteen-year-old senior at Crampton Prep school in Pennsylvania. Jamie is not well liked at his school. Whenever the cross-country team runs past him, someone yells, "Asshole!" And during a school production of *Romeo and Juliet*, his classmates cheer when he is run through with a sword while playing Mercutio. Later, at the cast party, Jamie stands off to the side and gazes at a pretty blonde. He is attracted to her, but he is shy and feels intimidated. Meanwhile, another student named Deedee tries to flirt with him, but he seems oblivious to her advances.

Jamie is a nice guy, but he lacks confidence. The strained relationships with his peers are made even more painful when a flashback—which occurs three years prior in New Jersey—details the close relationship between Jamie and his brother, Gerry. While Jamie is awkward and paranoid, Gerry is funny and warm. But after experimenting with LSD at his own school, during which he jumps out of his first-floor window, Gerry gets kicked out. In a tender moment of brotherly love, Gerry tries to convince Jamie to attend a good prep school so he can earn good grades and be successful. It's a moving scene that highlights the importance of family members who admit their own mistakes so those they love won't make the same ones.

It's clear that Jamie is immature, but after reading J. D. Salinger's classic coming-of-age novel *The Catcher in the Rye*, he decides to adapt the novel into a play for his independent study project. When asked why he has such a passion for this project, Jamie tells his teacher, "It spoke to me. . . . For the first time, I felt like I was reading about someone who understands me." His statement is a testament to the power of literature. Reading allows us to live vicariously through other characters and to experience their lives as our own. Feeling emboldened, Jamie hopes to perform the play at his school with himself in the lead role of Holden Caulfield. But first, he needs permission from the reclusive author, and no one seems to know where Salinger lives.

Jamie writes letters to several people who might know of Salinger's whereabouts, but his letters go unanswered. At one point, while in New York City for a drama competition, he sneaks off to a literary agency in the hope of securing Salinger's address. He is told, however, that Salinger doesn't want to see or speak to anyone. Eventually, Jamie thinks he's discovered the town in which Salinger lives. His plan is to travel to New Hampshire, locate J. D. Salinger, and receive permission to put on his theatrical adaptation of *The Catcher in the Rye*.

Jamie decides to hitchhike, but Deedee offers to drive him in her car because she likes adventures. Thus begins a funny and touching road trip in which Jamie and Deedee talk about books and school and engage each other in philosophical discussions. Away from their parents, they now have the opportunity to practice being adults, especially when they spend the night in a hotel. Wearing a ring, Jamie rents a room while pretending the two of them are married. But he is inexperienced with women and nervous about sex. His awkward reaction to Deedee's seduction is emblematic of how he handles conflict in his life. Rather than communicate and address his problems, Jamie avoids them and ends up isolating himself from those around him.

Upon arriving in the town, no one seems to know anything about J. D. Salinger. Some people claim to have never heard his name while others can't remember where his house is located. The townspeople send Jamie and Deedee on a wild goose chase in all directions. During an entire day, the two teenagers drive across the countryside—up and down hills, winding through one-lane country roads—while stopping periodically to ask if anyone knows where the famous author lives. The townspeople continue to feign ignorance until one man tells Jamie that he won't find Salinger because the author doesn't want to be found.

When Jamie does meet J. D. Salinger, he proudly tells him about the play he's adapted. But Salinger just shakes his head and tells him it's a terrible idea. Jamie is disheartened, but it's a sobering moment in which he realizes that personal and ambitious expectations are not always realistic or universal. Salinger is adamant that the novel shouldn't be interpreted and that it can't be done successfully. While this is certainly not the response for which Jamie was hoping, it is the catalyst that sets in motion the third act of the film in which Jamie will have to deal with certain truths he has been avoiding.

The film works well for those who have read *The Catcher in the Rye*. There are many parallels to specific events in the book, and several of the characters make statements and perform actions that are reminiscent of Holden Caulfield—for example, whenever Jamie turns toward the camera and breaks the fourth wall to speak directly to the viewer, assuming the same snarky tone and jaded opinions as Holden. But even those who have never read the book will still appreciate the story of a lonely teenager who is angry at the world and at himself.

Why You Should See This Film: Because it's a philosophical road trip filled with literary wisdom and poignant self-reflection.

Main Themes: Bullying * Jealousy * Rebelliousness * Death * Communication

Classic Line: "I really don't know how to talk to adults. They scare me."

Recommended Double Feature: *Dead Poets Society* (1989); Rated PG, 140 minutes, Drama

CORALINE
(2009)

Directed by: Henry Selick
Written by: Henry Selick, based on the novel by Neil Gaiman
Cast: Dakota Fanning (Coraline), Teri Hatcher (Mel/Other Mother), John Hodgman (Charlie/Other Father), Keith David (The Cat)
Rating: Rated PG for thematic elements, scary images, some language, and suggestive humor
Runtime: 100 minutes
Genre: Fantasy-horror-animation

The Gist: This stop-motion animated film focuses on a young girl named Coraline Jones who has just moved with her parents from Michigan to Oregon. Like most children on the verge of adolescence, Coraline fantasizes about a world without her parents. She imagines a world in which she is loved and praised all the time and allowed to do whatever she wants and whenever she wants. She is not the most likable girl, often acting bratty and huffy because she is bored and lonely. But that boredom soon turns into a thrilling adventure when she finds herself in a fantasy world and must rescue her parents from an evil woman.

Coraline's restlessness and curiosity are on display during the film's opening moments. She leaves her apartment to wander through a misty landscape while being followed by a black cat. She meets a boy nicknamed Wybie, and their conversation shows her to be plucky and confident, though somewhat rude. Her attitude partly stems from feeling abandoned at home. She doesn't like that her parents are always busy. They don't have time to play with her because they are working hard to meet their deadline for a garden catalog.

Later, while walking around her apartment, Coraline investigates closets and hallways. She peers into all of the nooks and crannies. She soon discovers a hidden door that reveals a long tunnel leading to another world. When she enters this fantasy realm, she discovers her Other Mother and her Other Father. These characters live in a grotesque world that darkly mirrors her own. In this world there are severed hands, the trapped souls of children, performing circus mice, and people who enjoy munching on black beetles. At first, Coraline does not recognize the creepiness of this other world. For her, this new landscape offers an exciting contrast to the drab life she lives with her parents.

The animation in this fantasy world is more colorful and sharp than the muted colors in the real world. They reflect the initial excitement and wonder that Coraline feels. But while the real world is less flashy, it also contains more genuine emotion. The fantasy world is mesmerizing and seductive, but it is also fake. The characters in this fantasy world entice her with promises and attention. They remind her how bored she is at home. They tell her that if she stays in the other world with them, then they will play with her all the time. The idea of being the center of attention is always enticing, and Coraline likes the thought of having whatever she wants and of not being neglected.

The Other Mother is the most powerful force in the fantasy world. She's an alternative version of Coraline's own mother and wants to claim Coraline as her own daughter. When Coraline asks the black cat why the Other Mother wants to keep her, it replies, "She wants something to love, I think. Something that isn't her. Or, maybe she'd just love something to eat." While the Other Mother seems doting and loving, and cooks delicious meals, she also smothers Coraline with love and attention. She treats her as if she were nothing more than an object. Coraline eventually realizes that her other home is not quite as fun and carefree as she initially thought. If she wants to eat the best food and play with the best toys, then it will come with a price.

To remain in the fantasy world, Coraline has to act in accordance with the Other Mother's wishes. She must allow her Other Parents to sew big black buttons onto her eyes. Naturally, she finds this idea repulsive.

Indeed, everyone in the fantasy world has the same expression because they all sport the black button eyes. As a result, they lack warmth and emotion. They lack an identity. When Coraline starts to act rebellious, showing her apprehension with the fantasy world, the Other Mother kidnaps Coraline's parents. With no one to protect her, Coraline must now depend on herself to rescue them.

The film deftly mixes humor and fright. It offers several intense moments as well as some heartfelt ones that reflect the importance of family. In presenting its spooky story of a resourceful girl who leaves the security of her home to battle monsters and become a hero, the film also pays homage to other children's classics such as *Alice's Adventures in Wonderland*, in which a young girl finds herself journeying through a fantastic other world, and *The Lion, the Witch and the Wardrobe* in which a strange portal connects our primary world with a secondary one.

By discovering clues and evading those who want to harm her—in rescuing her real parents and the ghost children—Coraline realizes that while her real parents have odd quirks and habits that bother her, she needs to accept that not everyone is perfect. Ultimately, she would rather live in an imperfect home with genuine love than live in a seemingly perfect home filled with false love and unrealistic expectations.

Why You Should See This Film: Because it's a creepy journey of self-discovery through a gothic fantasy world filled with eccentric characters and bizarre imagery.

Main Themes: Survival * Deception * Family * Courage * Oppression

Classic Line: "They say even the proudest spirit can be broken . . . with love."

Recommended Double Feature: *Spirited Away* (2001); Rated PG, 125 minutes, Fantasy-animation

DAZED AND CONFUSED
(1993)

Directed by: Richard Linklater
Written by: Richard Linklater
Cast: Jason London (Pink), Adam Goldberg (Mike), Matthew McConaughey (Wooderson), Anthony Rapp (Tony), Marissa Ribisi (Cynthia), Wiley Wiggins (Mitch)
Rating: Rated R for adult content, adult language, drug use, and mild violence
Runtime: 102 minutes
Genre: Comedy

The Gist: The film begins at Lee High school in Texas. It's the last day of school in 1976. As Aerosmith's classic rock tune "Sweet Emotion" plays during the opening scene, we're presented with a wide assortment of characters that typify the usual clichés: jocks, stoners, nerds, and preppy girls. There is excitement in the hallways and on the grounds, the kind of youthful exuberance that signals the end of a long school year and the anticipation of an entire summer. Taking place within a twenty-four-hour period, the film follows many of these teenagers as they celebrate, ruminate, fight, and drive around town in search of a good time.

Dazed and Confused presents a group of quirky and interesting characters and follows them through the rest of the afternoon, during a party-fueled night, and into the haze of an early morning. There is Pink, a star football player; Mitch, an incoming freshman who is nervous about beginning high school; a trio of close friends consisting of Tony, Cynthia, and Mike; a rowdy group of seniors who enjoy hazing the newbies; and Wooderson, a laid-back guy in his early twenties who still hangs out with the high school students.

Anyone who remembers the thrill of the last day of school will experience a wave of nostalgia as the final bell rings and the school erupts into chaos. As Alice Cooper sings "School's Out," all the students burst out of their classrooms. They empty their lockers and hurl fistfuls of paper into the air. They push open the doors, whooping and hollering as they rush outside into the bright sunlight. They're eager to begin their summer vacation and experience freedom from rules and regulations. In a sense, they're getting rid of the stress and expectations that have been heaped upon them by parents and teachers.

The incoming freshmen are subjected to embarrassing initiations by the upperclassmen. The boys are paddled with wooden boards decorated just for the occasion. The girls, after wearing pacifiers, are covered in ketchup and mustard and raw eggs and told to propose to random boys. The students' objectification emphasizes their perceived immaturity and the idea that they can't be considered "cool" until they've fulfilled these

Rory Cochrane, Matthew McConaughey. ***Gramercy Pictures/Photofest © Gramercy Pictures***

ridiculous tests of initiation. While these hazing ceremonies are yearly rituals in the town, they are also demeaning and embarrassing.

Amid the hazing and partying, there are also serious moments, such as when Cynthia tells Mike and Tony she would "like to stop thinking of the present as some minor, insignificant preamble to something else." And Pink struggles with deciding whether or not to sign a pledge promising that he won't drink or take drugs during the summer. While his teammates seem to have no problem with the coach's request, Pink feels like the athletics department is trying to control his life. He's upset by the limitations placed upon him. Then there's Mitch, who spends a good part of the film trying to dodge the upperclassmen who are out to paddle him and all of his friends.

Many of these students are wondering what comes next, whether it's going off to college, becoming a freshman, or facing another year at Lee High. They're looking for experiences, and part of the film's appeal is that there's no plot, just a bunch of stories that are connected by a great soundtrack and a group of teenagers who need to find a purpose in whatever they do. Mike says that everyone needs a visceral experience, and the loose structure of the film provides them with a variety of such experiences as they drive around town, engage in philosophical conversations, play pool at the Emporium, and meet in a field for a late-night keg party.

All of these characters, regardless of which clique they fall into, are familiar to us. We've sat next to them in class. We've seen them at the pep rallies and the football games. We understand the innocence and exhilaration that causes them to fight and argue and flirt, or to be daring and fall recklessly in love. At one point, Pink jokes that he hopes his high school years aren't the best years of his life. He finds that idea incredibly depressing. While his statement does seem overdramatic, it reflects a love/hate relationship for a time in our lives when we desperately want independence, even if we don't know what to do with it.

The final shot shows a car filled with teenagers as they speed down a highway in the early morning, on their way to purchase Aerosmith tickets. They smile and laugh, the road stretched out before them. They are driving away from everything familiar, racing toward the unknown and hoping that wherever they are going is a hell of a lot better than where they have been.

Why You Should See This Film: Because it's like climbing into a Corvette Stingray with a bunch of your closest friends and cruising around town with the music blasting.

Main Themes: Bullying * Conformity * Individuality * Rebelliousness * Courage

Classic Line: "That's what I love about these high school girls, man. I get older, they stay the same age."

Recommended Double Feature: *Everybody Wants Some!!* (2016); Rated R, 117 minutes, Comedy

EASY A
(2010)

Directed by: Will Gluck
Written by: Bert V. Royal
Cast: Emma Stone (Olive), Amanda Bynes (Marianne), Aly Michalka (Rhiannon), Penn Badgley (Todd)
Rating: Rated PG-13 for mature thematic elements involving teen sexuality, language, and some drug material
Runtime: 92 minutes
Genre: Romantic comedy

The Gist: Olive Penderghast is a seventeen-year-old high school student who lives in Ojai, California. She's smart, friendly, and good hearted, not to mention sassy. But her stable and easygoing life suddenly falls apart after she lies to her best friend (Rhiannon), and suddenly becomes popular in all the wrong ways. She fabricates a story about having sex with a college guy named George. In no time at all her story spreads like wildfire, growing more and more exaggerated, until Olive is the subject of cruel gossip at the hands of everyone, including horny losers, jocks who ogle her, and a radical church group led by the mean Marianne.

The elaborate story Olive tells Rhiannon about having sex is funny for several reasons. The awkward manner in which she tells it indicates she is making it all up. Also, the activities she describes in no way reflect her persona. Olive was actually at home all weekend. She danced and sang in her bedroom, painted her toes, and played with her dog. On some level, she seems embarrassed that she doesn't spend more time going to parties and pursuing boys, which is why she buckles under Rhiannon's insistence that her imaginary date turned into her first sexual encounter.

The entire film is narrated by Olive while she sits in her bedroom in front of her computer, speaking into her webcam. She feels guilty about lying to her friends and putting herself in awkward situations. Her confessional, which is equally hilarious and dramatic, is prompted not only by her newfound reputation as a tramp—which she perpetuates by her actions and choice of clothing—but also by her deepening attraction to Todd, a classmate whom she has known and liked since middle school.

Despite being called a skank by many of her classmates, Olive isn't a party girl. Instead of being a social butterfly, she hangs out with Rhiannon and spends time with her family, which consists of her mother, father, and an adopted younger brother. Her parents are the epitome of cool. They are funny, supportive, and open minded. As if illustrating the sweetness and charm of this close-knit unit, everyone in the household is named after a type of food: her father's name is Dill, her mother's name is Rosemary, and her brother's name is Chip.

Olive is a good student who cares a lot about other people. In fact, it's her kindness toward others that gets her into trouble. Once news of her exploits begin to spread, unpopular classmates approach her with various propositions. To them, she is their only hope of becoming cool. Tired of being bullied because they are gay, or because they are overweight, they ask her to lie about hooking up with them. In return, they give her gift cards to stores like Home Depot and the Gap.

Olive likes the attention she receives, relishing this new identity and the chance to play off her innocent nature. But when friendships are ruined and people try to take advantage of her, Olive realizes her lies have gone too far. She admits, "I was used to being by myself, but I had never felt more alone." Her actions remind us that adolescence is often a time of impulsivity. Some decisions are made without considering the consequences while others are given too much deliberation. Also, Olive's attempts to assist those who are being bullied and treated unfairly is admirable, but she shouldn't have to change who she is to do so.

This film is based loosely on Nathaniel Hawthorne's classic American novel *The Scarlet Letter*, which is required reading in many American high schools. As it so happens, this is the novel Olive is reading and discussing in her English class. Though Olive isn't cast off into the forest like Hester Prynne, she is taunted and alienated by her peers. And Marianne's group—spouting fire and brimstone dialogue and calling Olive a whore—are representative of those zealous Puritans who chastise Hester in the novel.

Olive channels her inner power by wearing provocative clothes and by stitching a scarlet "A" onto her dress—perhaps as a symbol to remind herself that she is genuinely a good person, or perhaps to make a statement about how people tend to label each other based on appearances and rumors. Olive's brashness promotes self-expression and individuality, but it also suggests the importance of understanding one's limitations. At first, Olive feels emboldened, strutting around the school with confidence and claiming the A stands for "Awesome," but as she continues to lie, her world spirals out of control until she's forced to take responsibility and fix the complicated situation she helped to create.

Why You Should See This Film: Because it's funny and fascinating to watch Puritan ideals adapted into a satirical story involving regret and reputation.

Main Themes: Honesty * Peer Pressure * Empowerment * Judgment * Conformity

Classic Line: "Just because you lost your virginity doesn't mean you can go around throwing your cat at everybody!"

Recommended Double Feature: *She's the Man* (2006); Rated PG-13, 105 minutes, Romantic comedy

THE EDGE OF SEVENTEEN
(2016)

Directed by: Kelly Fremon Craig
Written by: Kelly Fremon Craig
Cast: Hailee Steinfeld (Nadine), Woody Harrelson (Mr. Bruner), Blake Jenner (Darian), Haley Lu Richardson (Krista), Hayden Szeto (Erwin), Kyra Sedgwick (Mona)
Rating: Rated R for adult content and adult language
Runtime: 104 minutes
Genre: Comedy-drama

The Gist: Nadine is a seventeen-year-old, quirky high school junior who lives with her mother (Mona) and older brother (Darian) in the suburbs of Portland, Oregon. Her father died of a heart attack several years earlier, a tragedy that has fractured the family. Their days are now punctuated with bickering and resentment, their anger erupting in a series of arguments that reveal the characters' need for love and affection. Nadine has no friends except for her best friend Krista. Darian, however, is handsome and popular. He also functions as the man of the house, trying to keep the peace between Nadine and Mona.

Nadine is bursting with angst, and her voice-over at the beginning of the film is a type of confessional that will occur throughout the film. We learn about her stubborn nature and how lonely she is. We learn about the jealousy she feels toward Darian, the turbulent relationship she experiences with her mother, and the positive relationship she enjoyed with her father. These personal moments illustrate Nadine's need to communicate with other people, even if she doesn't always know how to do so.

Nadine informs her English teacher, Mr. Bruner, that she plans to kill herself. She delivers this information not in a tragic manner, but in a sharp and witty way that demonstrates how much she wants to be acknowledged. She tells Mr. Bruner that she doesn't want to make people watch her die, but whichever way she kills herself should be a spectacle. Her flippant and egotistical remarks contribute to some of the film's funniest moments, illustrating the point that our lives are a combination of humor and pathos. She knows she is weird and awkward—whether feeling like an outcast at a party or while flirting with an older student she has a crush on—but the fact that she talks with Mr. Bruner about her problems on a regular basis suggests that her dark thoughts are not meant to be taken seriously. Instead, they reflect her desire to be part of a social group and to experience a normal teenage lifestyle.

Likewise, Mr. Bruner's glib responses to Nadine's constant confessions are funny in their brutal honesty. He's an authority figure who's expected to show concern, but when she tells him she doesn't have any friends, and how much she dislikes her entire generation, he pauses for

Hailee Steinfeld, Hayden Szeto. *STX Entertainment/Photofest © STX Entertainment*

a moment and says, "Maybe . . . nobody likes you." His unwillingness to encourage her self-pity reveals that he cares for her, especially because he doesn't yell at her or ridicule her whenever she interrupts his lunch break.

We all understand that our days can swing from good to bad in a matter of seconds, which helps us relate to Nadine as she wanders through her days on a journey of self-discovery. She tries to appear strong while battling with unhappiness, and at one point she says, "I had the worst thought: I've got to spend the rest of my life with myself." This moment is a step toward improving the various relationships with her family members, as well as an awareness that she is partly responsible for her misery, having made several bad choices and selfish decisions.

When Darian and Krista start dating, Nadine finds herself bitter and all alone. She forces Krista to choose between her and her brother, and she's upset when Krista refuses. This conflict reminds us how important intimacy is during adolescence. Rather than discard old friendships to start new ones, it's important that teenagers learn how to balance all the different relationships in their lives. Krista, who is clearly the more mature of the two girls, stands firm. She wants to maintain both her friendship with Nadine and her budding relationship with Darian, which forces Nadine to seek out others for attention.

One of those people is Erwin Kim, a fellow classmate who has a crush on Nadine. Like Nadine, Erwin is lonely—though in a physical way compared to Nadine's emotional solitude—and their friendship slowly morphs from simply talking in English class to swimming together in his pool and riding the Ferris wheel at a carnival. Erwin's interactions with Nadine are sweet and good natured, even though he is often tongue tied around her. There is a relaxed atmosphere between the two of them that serves as a needed calm in her tempestuous life.

The film's mood is comical and touching, realistic in its depiction of family issues and adolescent hardships. The characters are also complex and true to life, possessing good and bad attributes that elicit our compassion and help us to understand their struggles. Toward the end of the film, Nadine's mom offers her daughter some poignant advice about remembering that there are lots of miserable people in the world, and that practicing empathy can often lead to self-improvement. Mona's advice highlights the need for Nadine to be more active in fixing the problems in her life rather than constantly bitching about how unfair they are.

Why You Should See This Film: Because it's an accurate portrayal of a self-absorbed teen who struggles with her social life and a dysfunctional family.

Main Themes: Depression * Family * Rebelliousness * Selfishness * Communication

Classic Line: "There are two types of people in this world: the people who naturally excel at life. And the people who hope all those people die in a big explosion."

Recommended Double Feature: *Turn Me On, Dammit!* (2011); Not Rated, 76 minutes, Comedy-romance

EIGHTH GRADE

(2018)

Directed by: Bo Burnham
Written by: Bo Burnham
Cast: Elsie Fisher (Kayla), Josh Hamilton (Mark), Emily Robinson (Olivia), Luke Prael (Aiden)
Rating: Rated R for language and some sexual material
Runtime: 93 minutes
Genre: Drama

The Gist: Here is a film so realistic in its representation of teenage life that it sometimes feels more like a documentary than a feature film. Often funny, and occasionally sad—but almost always cringeworthy—*Eighth Grade* depicts the anxieties of trying to fit in, as well as the challenges of living in a society where relationships depend so much on social media. Also, the R rating is completely undeserved. The language and content is more representative of a PG-13 film.

Kayla Day is thirteen years old and drifting through her last week of eighth grade. Amid the kids sniffing markers and playing with their braces, she sits by herself, quietly observing everyone around her. She is shy and doesn't talk much at school. Despite her silence, Kayla claims she's a social person. She creates a series of YouTube videos focusing on topics like "being yourself," "putting yourself out there," and "how to be confident." Talking to a computer screen supplies her with a sense of power and self-assurance, and in addressing her viewers—of which there are very few—she is also building up the motivation to approach her peers, especially the popular Aiden, on whom she has a big crush.

She lives with her father, and their relationship consists of him struggling to talk with her while she plays on her iPhone and ignores him. She listens to music at the dinner table, staring down at the bright screen while texting and playing games. Whenever her father asks her a question, she reacts with a display of overdramatic frustration. Kayla has reached an age where it's not fashionable to spend time with one's parents. She's beginning to look at boys in a more sexual way, and she views her home life as stifling. Her father—who demonstrates a considerable amount of patience with his teenage daughter—seems unsure how to handle her indifference, though he continuously tells her how special and awesome he thinks she is.

For Kayla and her classmates, life exists in the cloud and on the internet. She is constantly plugged into social media, obsessed with messaging and staying current on everything her classmates are saying and doing. Whether lying in bed at night or walking through the hallway in between her classes, Kayla clutches her phone like a lifeline. She and her classmates insert "like" into every sentence and spend so much time on their iPhones that they rarely engage in eye-to-eye contact when speaking with another person. Since Kayla doesn't have many friends, her YouTube videos function as a way of feeling included.

When she's invited to a birthday party, she is both excited and horrified. She doesn't have many friends. She feels uncomfortable striking up conversations with the popular kids, but she also realizes the social importance of this event. When she arrives at the house, however, she has a panic attack in the bathroom while putting on her swimsuit. She is embarrassed and tongue tied the entire time, particularly when the girls gather for a group picture or when Aiden walks into the room and engages her in a conversation.

Kayla is constantly nervous because she doesn't want to feel excluded. She compares her emotions to the uneasy feeling people often get while waiting in line to ride a roller coaster. She says, "I get that all the time. And then I never get the feeling of after you ride the roller coaster." She has high expectations for herself, as evidenced by a time capsule she opens during the film, one that she put together in sixth grade. Watching herself on video—asking the future version of herself all sorts of questions about who her current friends are in middle school, and if she has a serious boyfriend—it's apparent that she's disappointed in herself for not taking more chances. And though she understands that she needs to be more assertive and composed, she also realizes the importance of not changing who she is just to impress other people.

But Kayla's life improves when she participates in a high school shadow program and meets Olivia, a twelfth grader who befriends her. And when Olivia invites Kayla to meet up with her and her friends at the mall, it's hard not to smile at the happiness Kayla feels at finally being included. The opportunity to hang out with older students at the food court provides her with a glimpse of high school life and more adult conversations, including an uncomfortable game of truth or dare in the backseat of a car. These experiences push Kayla to better herself, whether enjoying a heartfelt talk with her father in their backyard or making a list of goals that includes gaining more confidence and finding a best friend.

Eighth Grade is a reminder of how awkward and traumatic growing up can be, and of how alone we sometimes feel while navigating the rocky terrain of adolescence. It also illustrates how technology places intense pressure on young adults. Not only do they worry about whether they should post on social media, they also worry about what to post and when to post it. This persistent stress can lead to naïve expectations regarding friendships and popularity. Plus, it's difficult to establish a self-identity when you're trying so hard to be exactly like everyone else.

Why You Should See This Film: Because it perfectly captures the angst and confusion of being a thirteen-year-old who's battling hormones and insecurities.

Main Themes: Self-Confidence * Acceptance * Insecurity * Love * Obsession

Classic Line: "Just cause things are happening to you right now doesn't mean that they're always going to happen to you."

Recommended Double Feature: *Thirteen* (2003); Rated R, 100 minutes, Drama

FAST TIMES AT RIDGEMONT HIGH
(1982)

Directed by: Amy Heckerling
Written by: Cameron Crowe, based on his book *Fast Times at Ridgemont High: A True Story*
Cast: Sean Penn (Spicoli), Jennifer Jason Leigh (Stacy), Judge Reinhold (Brad), Phoebe Cates (Linda), Brian Backer (Mark), Robert Romanus (Mike)
Rating: Rated R for language, nudity, drug use, and sexual situations
Runtime: 90 minutes
Genre: Comedy-drama

The Gist: The key to the film is right there in the title. These are fast times, indeed, a streaking blur of fast food, fast cars, and fast money that all present high school as a madcap adventure full of relationships, pep rallies, and lusting after crushes. From its opening scenes set in a rowdy mall, the camera zooming every which way to show a variety of fashions and flirtations, the film captures perfectly the excitement and frustration inherent in adolescence, whether it's losing one's virginity, trying to pass history class, or enduring a crappy part-time job.

The film focuses on a diverse group of characters over the course of one school year, including Jeff Spicoli (the token surfer dude), Stacy Hamilton (the innocent and naïve virgin), Brad Hamilton (a poster boy for anyone who has ever hated working in a restaurant), Mike Damone (a smooth-talking scalper whose relationship advice is, "When it comes

Brian Backer, Jennifer Jason Leigh. ***MCA/Universal Pictures/Photofest © MCA–Universal***

down to making out, whenever possible, put on side one of *Led Zeppelin IV*"), Mark Ratner (a shy and awkward boy who lacks self-confidence), and Linda Barrett (the sexually experienced senior whose bikini scene will live in infamy).

Part of the fun in watching the film is observing how characters socialize within their own private circles, exhibiting a certain comfort and cliquish language, such as when Stacy tells Linda she wants a relationship and Linda responds by lamenting the fact that no one can get cable TV in Ridgemont. The banter among the characters is fresh and honest, but it also demonstrates an inexperience in regard to their understanding of the adult world. And it's equally enjoyable to see these characters break free from their socially constructed boundaries to interact with each other. Sometimes, it's incredibly uncomfortable while other times a conversation reveals a growing tolerance and rapport. As with most teenagers, the characters in *Fast Times at Ridgemont High* talk to others not just because they want to be heard and respected, but because they want to reaffirm what they think they already know.

The lack of a cohesive plot is part of the story's appeal. The film is an assortment of funny and dramatic vignettes. Who can forget the look on the teacher's face when Spicoli orders a pizza and has it delivered during class? Or when an obnoxious customer tells Brad his order is 100 percent guaranteed and Brad threatens to kick his ass? These are characters who tend to speak before they think. It's clear that such actions have positive and negative consequences, whether it's having to find a new job or sacrificing free time to pass history class.

A significant message in the film is the importance of being respectful toward others and of communicating effectively. This is especially important during an age when students are learning to manage their responsibilities, whether with their part-time jobs or their budding relationships. In fact, the film's more serious moments—concerning drug use, teen pregnancy, and abortion—highlight the adult themes and issues that can creep into high school life. But like all great coming-of-age films, the viewer can live vicariously through these characters and learn the proper way to both act and react in certain situations.

The film's humorous scenes also remind us that high school is a tumultuous time in which our emotions can fluctuate wildly between happiness and depression, between eagerness and apprehension. One class period or quick trip to the mall, one heated conversation with another student or a teacher, can ruin a great morning or complicate an uneventful afternoon. The film's emphasis on so many different characters, and on the wide range of emotions they constantly display, is a testament to the uncertainty that most high schoolers experience on a daily basis, the knowledge that they are not always in control, that their lives are unpredictable, and that their happiness and security is often contingent upon others.

Yet, despite the numerous conflicts and struggles, there's a sweetness lurking just below the film's surface, an innocence that offsets the hip profanity and naïve sexuality that we tend to encounter in the hallways of almost every high school. Brad agrees not to tell his parents about the flowers his sister received from an older man; there is a heartfelt one-on-one session between Spicoli and a teacher that reveals a tenderness and maturity in both characters; and Mark confronts Mike about his treatment of Stacy, illustrating not only his true feelings for her, but that he has grown more confident and self-assured.

And who can forget the soundtrack? Tom Petty singing "American Girl," the Go-Go's singing "We Got the Beat," and Jackson Browne belting out "Somebody's Baby." The music itself is upbeat and lively, capturing not only the energy of the early 1980s, but symbolizing the enthusiasm and reckless abandon with which these troubled characters barrel through the highs and lows of another academic year.

Why You Should See This Film: Because it's a winning mixture of teen angst coupled with stoner vibes and sexual discovery.

Main Themes: Responsibility * Judgment * Innocence * Communication * Individuality

Classic Line: "I can see it all now, this is gonna be just like last summer. You fell in love with that girl at the Fotomat, you bought forty dollars' worth of fuckin' film, and you never even talked to her. You don't even own a camera."

Recommended Double Feature: *Cooley High* (1975); Rated PG, 107 minutes, Drama-comedy

FERRIS BUELLER'S DAY OFF
(1986)

Directed by: John Hughes
Written by: John Hughes
Cast: Matthew Broderick (Ferris), Alan Ruck (Cameron), Mia Sara (Sloane), Jennifer Grey (Jeanie), Jeffrey Jones (Rooney)
Rating: Rated PG-13 for language and sexual references
Runtime: 103 minutes
Genre: Comedy-drama

The Gist: Ferris Bueller is a high school senior who wakes up one sunny morning and decides he doesn't want to go to school. After setting up an elaborate hoax, he drives a Ferrari into Chicago with his girlfriend (Sloane) and his best friend (Cameron). During the course of their fun-filled day, Ferris sings "Twist and Shout" while riding in a parade float, catches a foul ball at a Cubs game, and visits Willis Tower and the Art Institute of Chicago. Meanwhile, Edward Rooney—who is the dean of students—suspects Ferris is playing hooky and tries to nail him in the act.

Ferris is an easy character to root for. He's endearing because he's an adolescent trickster who is charismatic and self-assured. He's also one of the most popular students in the school, a point made early in the film when one of the characters says, "The sportos, the motorheads, geeks, sluts, bloods, wastoids, dweebies, dickheads . . . they all adore him. They think he's a righteous dude." Part of his appeal lies in the way that he looks directly into the camera and breaks the fourth wall to address the viewer, like when he explains how to fake out one's parents with clammy hands. His confidence is so infectious that it's easy to support him as he embarks on his mission to have a great time, no matter how difficult or far-fetched it might seem.

The film is realistic in depicting serious issues. Cameron has a distant and difficult relationship with his parents. Ferris fights with his sister, Jeanie, who hates the attention her brother receives and would love to see him punished for ditching school. Each of these characters is certainly naïve and impulsive. But one of the joys of the film is that they are often smarter and more thoughtful than the adults. For instance, Edward Rooney is fooled into releasing Sloane from school. And Ferris's parents check on him throughout the day without realizing there's a mannequin in his bed accompanied by an audio recording of loud snores.

In many ways, though, the film is also a fantasy. Because Ferris Bueller is more than a character. He's a symbol for freedom. He's someone who has decided to start living now instead of waiting until after he graduates from high school. Ferris acts the way we wish we could act in real life. He's fearless while impersonating Abe Froman, the sausage king of Chicago, when the three friends decide to each lunch at the ritzy Chez Quis. He fools his parents into believing he's sick by acting faint and listless with outstretched hands and raspy breaths. And when his parents order him to stay home and rest, Ferris feigns concern in a test he has that day. He tells them he needs to take the test so he can get into a good college and live a fruitful life.

Ferris avoids getting caught multiple times throughout the film. He always flashes a winning smile and maintains his cool composure. In turn, he is treated with respect and admiration by his peers. A water tower reads "Save Ferris" in huge black letters; the English faculty members send him flowers; and a police officer tells Ferris's mom to let him know that all the officers at the station are pulling for him. The consideration that Ferris receives is the same attention many adolescents wish to receive from their peers, as well as from adults. Most of us want to believe that our words and actions are valued by others. Ferris is the sun around which everyone in his vicinity orbits, and it's hard not to feel jealous when we're watching him navigate with such ease and humor across an adolescent terrain that is typically so rocky and unpredictable.

Ferris Bueller lives his life to the fullest, and he teaches us to make the most of every day. He's got hold of the "carpe" in one hand and the "diem" in the other, and he's constantly thinking about the future rather than bitching about the present. He suggests that there's more to be learned outside of high school, as indicated by the round-trip journey the three characters take, both physically and emotionally. Ferris shows us that the best experiences are oftentimes the ones we create for ourselves. He is honest in his feelings and intentions, and if some of his actions seem immature—like when he plays "The Blue Danube" on his keyboard using assorted coughs and sick sounds—then at least they aren't malicious and mean spirited.

It also becomes clear that Ferris has skipped school because he wants to get Cameron out of bed and show him a good time. Ferris is worried about his friend's mental health, which shows us a selfless side of his character while highlighting the value of true friendship. And if Ferris is the larger-than-life icon who fuels our dreams of popularity and success, then it's Cameron who speaks realistically for any teenager who has ever felt unpopular and unloved, especially when he tells Ferris with the utmost confidence, "I'm gonna take a stand. And I'm gonna defend it. Right or wrong, I'm gonna defend it." In that moment, he reminds us that it's important to not only have a unique voice but to use it with conviction and whenever necessary.

Why You Should See This Film: Because it's a poignant shot of anti-authority mixed with a touch of philosophical whimsy.

Main Themes: Rebelliousness * Self-Confidence * Deception * Depression * Authority

Classic Line: "I do have a test today, that wasn't bullshit. It's on European socialism. I mean, really, what's the point? I'm not European. I don't plan on being European. So, who gives a crap if they're socialists? They could be fascist anarchists, it still doesn't change the fact that I don't own a car."

Recommended Double Feature: *House Party* (1990); Rated R, 102 minutes, Comedy-musical

FLIRTING
(1991)

Directed by: John Duigan
Written by: John Duigan
Cast: Noah Taylor (Danny), Thandie Newton (Thandiwe), Nicole Kidman (Nicola), Bartholomew Rose (Gilbert), Marshall Napier (Mr. Elliott)
Rating: Rated R for brief nudity and mild sexual content
Runtime: 99 minutes
Genre: Drama-romance

The Gist: This film centers on two intelligent teenagers who meet and fall in love while attending separate boarding schools in New South Wales, Australia, in 1965. The all-boys school is St. Albans; the all-girls school—which is located directly across the lake—is Cirencester Ladies College. Aside from the usual adolescent themes like sexuality and friendship, *Flirting* comments on race and politics. The two main characters, Danny and Thandiwe, are an interracial couple who must contend with not only their classmates' prejudices, but with world events that intrude upon their burgeoning romance.

Danny, who is from Australia, attends St. Albans. He is reprimanded by his teachers and bullied by his classmates. The students make fun of his occasional stuttering and call him "Bird" because he's scrawny. Danny's only friend is Gilbert, another quiet and introspective student who stands up for his friend in several key moments. Thandiwe, who is from Uganda, attends Cirencester Ladies College. She is studying at the college because her father is lecturing at a university in Canberra for one year. Like Danny, Thandiwe is excluded from the rest of her classmates. She has only a few close friends and is often teased by her classmates.

The opening scene introduces us to Danny as he stands in line with a bunch of his classmates. They are waiting to be caned by Mr. Elliott, one of the teachers. Whatever they did to earn this punishment is never revealed, but it's clear that harsh punishment is routine at St. Albans. Later, after the boys drop their pants to compare the bright red welts, Danny lies in bed and reflects on the struggles inherent in attending boarding school. Students either become part of the social group—which means they sacrifice their own individuality—or they retreat inside themselves and watch everything from an anxious and lonesome perspective.

But the view of Cirencester from Danny's bedroom window is a source of solace and inspiration. He compares both schools to two brooding volcanoes, which suggests the simmering sexual energy of the students. The two schools frequently meet for dances and debates. During these times, the students tend to stand at opposite ends of the room so they can size each other up. They whisper to each other while they choose their intended target, and then they proceed to flirt incessantly.

Thandie Newton, Noah Taylor. ***Samuel Goldwyn Films/Photofest © Samuel Goldwyn Films***

The students' lack of experience with the opposite sex renders these scenes comical and awkward, but also realistic.

Danny and Thandiwe first meet at a rugby match. She and two of her friends wander through the crowd, feigning interest in the game. Her friends are searching for potential boyfriends. Danny tells them the rugby match is a form of mating ritual. His blunt comment, and their ensuing conversation, piques Thandiwe's interest because she realizes he is an intellectual. Later, during a debate, they both argue against their own side's position, which draws them even closer together. She enjoys his argument for why rugby is the highest form of human endeavor and why it embodies the noblest virtues. He is impressed by her satirical explanation of rock-and-roll music as an intellectual pursuit.

They are both stubborn and rebellious. Together, they agree that their schools are like prisons. When they meet at a dance, they decide to skip the event and instead go to Danny's dormitory where they engage in a philosophical conversation about marriage and the art of communication. During the course of the film, Thandiwe tells Danny about her life in Africa. She reveals that her mother was killed and her father writes books about African nationalism. She tells him about struggles in the Belgian Congo and Angola. Danny has never heard of these places, saying, "I often think how all of us were going through the normal grubby business of school and growing up while the most incredible things were happening in her world." He realizes that all he knows about Africa comes from Tarzan comics and Hollywood movies. Their heartfelt conversations help to broaden his perspective on the world.

Danny recognizes how certain events have shaped Thandiwe's strength and character. And it's also inspiring to see how Danny and Thandiwe's relationship impacts those around them. Nicola, a prefect at Cirencester, acts withdrawn and standoffish, but she secretly admires Thandiwe's defiance and carefree attitude. Eventually, they grow to respect each other and share secrets. Likewise, Danny's determination to be with Thandiwe emboldens Gilbert to stand up for his friend when another student steals Danny's letter from Thandiwe and reads it aloud.

Flirting is smart and witty. It shows likable teenagers who struggle with their personal decisions. Their romance develops naturally, and every decision is an important one, especially given the expectations and limitations that are constantly placed upon them by the school administrators.

In some ways, Thandiwe provides Danny with a better education than St. Albans.

Why You Should See This Film: Because it's a romantic and life-affirming film about intelligent people falling in love and growing up.

Main Themes: Rebelliousness * Empathy * Conformity * Sexual Discovery * Authority

Classic Line: "People like to have someone to look down on. Makes them feel better about themselves."

Recommended Double Feature: *The Year My Voice Broke* (1987); Rated PG-13, 103 minutes, Drama-romance

HEATHERS
(1988)

Directed by: Michael Lehmann
Written by: Daniel Waters
Cast: Winona Ryder (Veronica), Christian Slater (J.D.), Shannen Doherty (Heather), Lisanne Falk (Heather), Kim Walker (Heather)
Rating: Rated R for profanity, strong sexual language, violence, alcohol and drug use, sexual situations, and smoking
Runtime: 103 minutes
Genre: Black comedy

The Gist: This is a morbid exploration of high school cliques that succeeds in disturbing us while simultaneously making us laugh out loud. The Heathers (composed of Heather Chandler, Heather Duke, Heather McNamara, and Veronica Sawyer) are the most powerful clique at Westerburg High School. While all of the Heathers are wealthy and pretty, Veronica is the only one who shows friendliness and compassion toward her fellow classmates. Her vacillating affection and disdain for her best friends is evident when she admits that she actually doesn't like them very much.

The Heathers are cruel and selfish girls. They value and celebrate themselves based on the power and superiority they exert over the students they bully on a daily basis. During the opening credits, the three Heathers trample flowers and play a game of croquet in which they aim the ball at Veronica's head. This scene shows that while Veronica is part of the Heathers, she is still an outsider. The Heathers walk around a beautiful manicured garden, dressed like posh students at a boarding school. With their red ribbons and red skirts—not to mention their copies of *Moby Dick* and *The Bell Jar*—they seem preppy and elitist, but they are also malicious and vindictive. They're willing to blackmail and embarrass anyone who challenges their authority.

Then there is Jason Dean, also known as J.D. He is Veronica's psycho boyfriend. He wears all black and decides to purge the school of the popular snobs by killing them and making the murders look like suicides. His name suggests two famous men associated with young adults, namely, J. D. Salinger (celebrated author of *The Catcher in the Rye*) and James Dean (an actor whose classic film *Rebel without a Cause* centers on rebellious and emotionally confused teenagers). The film presents J.D. as a mentally unbalanced young man who is more intelligent and contemplative than many of his classmates. He spouts clever one-liners and offers philosophical reasons for his murderous actions.

Yet despite the bullying and the bulimia, despite the shootings and the explosions, the film is very funny. It uses humor to poke fun at serious issues like depression and teen suicide. In one scene, a girl in the background is being sexually assaulted, but the moment takes on a darkly comic under-

Winona Ryder. *New World Pictures/Photofest © New World Pictures*

tone as Veronica displays boredom and irritation at having been dragged on a double date with two members of the football team who think a romantic evening involves getting drunk and tipping over cows.

Heather Chandler, who is the first to die, becomes even more popular after her death, a fact that baffles Veronica to no end, especially when she learns that Heather's suicide note will be featured in the yearbook. And it's clear that most of the students respond to Heather's suicide not because they liked her, but because they think it's the cool and acceptable thing to do. Heather's death is something to talk about, and it shows how people will exploit a tragedy to serve their own needs and desires. Students begin to wonder if they ever really knew Heather Chandler. And in their quest to be seen and acknowledged, they try to ascribe some meaning to her life. In doing so, however, they only appear shallow and selfish.

Throughout the film, Veronica writes in her diary. Her entries are communicated to the audience by voice-over, and the technique is effective because it feels like Veronica is confessing to everyone who's watching the movie. Her anger and sadness and frustration, coupled with her furious scribbling, allow her to become a more sympathetic character. We can all relate to moments when we went against our better judgment because we were afraid of how we might look in the eyes of those more popular.

And where are the parents? When they ask questions, their conversations feel more like a daily obligation than a show of genuine interest. Even the school staff is unemotional when learning about the deaths. Instead of caring about the students and providing counselors, they debate how much time off the students should receive. Upon hearing news of Heather Chandler's death, one teacher remarks, "I must say I was impressed to see that she made proper use of the word 'myriad' in her suicide note." All the adults in the film are distant and unsupportive. They seem to neither know nor care what is going on in their children's lives.

Heathers shows us the dark side of high school. One of the reasons the film is just as relevant today as it was in the 1980s is because violence in American schools has only increased. And while the film doesn't preach or spout a particular message, its sharp satire does suggest that the blame lies not just with students, but with parents, administrators, and even society as a whole. So we laugh and we cringe, we feel heartened and disgusted, and we empathize with Veronica when she wishes her high school could be a nice place.

Why You Should See This Film: Because it's a suicidal satire fueled by an onslaught of peer pressure and popularity.

Main Themes: Death * Obsession * Depression * Power * Disillusionment

Classic Line: "Dear Diary: My teen angst bullshit now has a body count."

Recommended Double Feature: *Donnie Darko* (2001); Rated R, 133 minutes, Drama-fantasy

HUNT FOR THE WILDERPEOPLE
(2016)

Directed by: Taika Waititi
Written by: Taika Waititi, based on the novel *Wild Pork and Watercress* by Barry Crump
Cast: Sam Neill (Hec), Julian Dennison (Ricky), Rima Te Wiata (Bella), Rachel House (Paula)
Rating: Rated PG-13 for some violent content and some language
Runtime: 101 minutes
Genre: Adventure-comedy-drama

The Gist: This New Zealand film is an absolute delight. Ricky Baker is a juvenile delinquent from the city who is sent to live on a remote farm with Bella and her husband, Hec. Described as "a real bad egg" by Paula, his child welfare services officer, Ricky's crimes amount to such petty activities as running away, spitting, throwing rocks, loitering, and kicking stuff. However, Ricky is actually a sweet kid whose mother abandoned him when he was born, and it's clear that what Ricky needs is not rehabilitation but a loving family.

Initially, Ricky is not charmed by his new rural setting, choosing to creep out of the house in the middle of the night and run away. He doesn't get very far, and when Bella wakes him up in a field she is more amused than angry. She assures him he can run away after breakfast. This indifference to Ricky's behavior is exactly what he needs. Had she punished him or admonished him for fleeing, he might have become more defiant and withdrawn. Instead, Bella has allowed Ricky some freedom, which establishes a sense of trust between them.

It's during his time on Bella and Hec's farm that Ricky learns what it means to be valued and supported. He has his own room stocked with several books, his birthday is acknowledged, and he helps out with random chores. For the first time in his life, Ricky feels like he has been accepted, and the most important symbol during this period is a red water bottle that Bella tucks into Ricky's bed every night. It shows Ricky that he is respected and loved, and the warmth it provides is the comfort and stability he has desired for so long. His joy and appreciation of this gesture is apparent every night when he smiles and holds the water bottle tight against his chest.

But when a tragedy occurs, Ricky runs away into the bush rather than be picked up by child welfare services. Lost and unable to survive on his own, he is found by Hec. Adding to their trouble is the misunderstanding that Hec has kidnapped Ricky. The two of them are then forced to live in the bush, and their constant bickering shows a deep divide between two people who have relied on only themselves for so long. Now, they must learn how to put their trust in others.

The rest of the film follows their adventures and misadventures. These are presented as a deft combination of slapstick moments, heartfelt conversations, and humorous escapes from their pursuers. *Hunt for the Wilderpeople* is broken up into ten chapters with titles like "Broken Foot Camp" and "War." In structuring the film into episodes, the director creates a steady rhythm that engages the viewer. With the introduction of each new chapter, the stakes increase as more conflicts arise, both externally and within the characters themselves. As well, each chapter feels like a short story with a beginning, a middle, and an end. This structure makes it easier to compartmentalize the major themes and conflicts in the film, especially during the scenes in which Ricky and Hec must embrace the concept of teamwork while learning to rely on each other.

The relationship between Ricky and Hec is the heart of the film. They forge a deep friendship, try to avoid being captured, and encounter a colorful group of characters. Both of them have experienced heartache and loneliness, and that common bond allows them to communicate openly with each other as they hike through the woods and wade across streams. Together, they forage for food and argue over whether or not "majesti-

Julian Dennison, Sam Neill. *The Orchard/Photofest* © *The Orchard*

cal" is a word. And the more time they spend together, the more they respect each other and begin to enjoy each other's company. When Hec tells Ricky that he and Bella couldn't have children, Ricky says, "That's not very fair. Some people can't even have babies, and the ones who can, they don't even want them." Such tender and sincere moments like this one are sprinkled throughout the film, and the truthful manner in which the characters speak is one of the reasons they are so likable and relatable.

While not everyone has been abandoned in his or her life, we all know what it feels like to be ignored and judged unfairly. We recognize the need to spend time alone because we believe there is no one else who understands us. Ricky's journey through the forest and over the mountains is a learning experience as Hec teaches him how to survive alone in the vast wilderness, which amounts to three important lessons: find water, go to higher ground, and don't get naked.

The key to staying alive is "the knack," which Hec describes to Ricky as a set of skills that helps to foster responsibility and to develop self-sufficiency. It becomes clear, though, that the knack is many things. It's common sense and patience; it's intuition and compassion. The knack is something we use every day of our lives, and not just when we're lost in the woods and trying to find our way back home. For Ricky and Hec, their time in the bush is proof that sometimes in life you need to get lost in order to find yourself.

Why You Should See This Film: Because it's a majestical film in which an extended camping trip becomes a heartfelt journey toward honesty and self-acceptance.

Main Themes: Survival * Friendship * Trust * Family * Teamwork

Classic Line: "Uncle, you're basically a criminal now. But on the bright side, you're famous."

Recommended Double Feature: *Boy* (2010); Not Rated, 90 minutes, Comedy-drama

IGBY GOES DOWN
(2002)

Directed by: Burr Steers
Written by: Burr Steers
Cast: Kieran Culkin (Igby), Susan Sarandon (Mimi), Jeff Goldblum (D.H.), Claire Danes (Sookie), Amanda Peet (Rachel), Bill Pullman (Jason)
Rating: Rated R for language, brief nudity, sexual content, and drug use
Runtime: 98 minutes
Genre: Black comedy–drama

The Gist: Igby Slocumb is a seventeen-year-old version of Holden Caulfield. He's smart, sarcastic, and rebellious, not to mention he's pissed off at the entire world. His family is wealthy, which he rebels against throughout the entire film. Igby has been kicked out of several prep schools and lives to disappoint his older brother (Oliver) and his mother, whom both children refer to as Mimi. That they don't call her "Mom" illustrates the lack of emotion exhibited among all three of them. Igby's father (Jason) has been committed to an institution because of mental health issues. To assert that Igby's family is dysfunctional would be a gross understatement.

Having been kicked out of prep school, and having run away from a military academy, Igby endures a stint at Clipped Wings: Teenage Wellness and Redirection Center. Because he's happily failing school, Igby is sent to New York City for the summer to work for his godfather (D.H.) as part of a construction crew that renovates high-class apartments. D.H. is a wealthy real estate tycoon whose entire life revolves around making money. He tells Igby that families should be run like companies. This philosophy—which focuses on material growth rather than on emotional growth—sets Igby apart from the adults in his life. He is especially distant from Oliver, who is studying economics at Columbia University. Igby wants to be defined by his own actions and beliefs, not on wealth and status that have been handed down to him by his family.

Igby's odyssey through New York during the rest of the summer, and his encounters with several different characters, is reminiscent of Holden Caulfield's journey through the same city in J. D. Salinger's classic novel *The Catcher in the Rye*. He meets Rachel, his godfather's mistress, who is a drug addict. Later, at a party, he meets a girl named Sookie Sapperstein. She is another lost soul who is taking a semester off from Bennington College because she needs to recuperate from "Entenmann's cookies, beer, diet pills, tension." Igby's friendship with Sookie is one of the more honest relationships in the film because he considers her a true friend and is willing to confide in her.

Igby has no direction because he has been given no direction. What he has been given is money and opportunities, many of which he didn't want and didn't ask for. His wealthy family has spent money and time trying to shape Igby into the person they want him to be rather than to let him make his own choices. He grew up watching his mother and father fight constantly. He also feels inadequate because he lives in his brother's shadow. The more fiercely his family pushes Igby to conform, the more intensely he revolts.

Igby's father once told his son that he felt overwhelmed by the world, and that he felt a great pressure bearing down on him. Igby now feels this same pressure. He is struggling to live up to his family's expectations. Because of this burden, he doesn't know how to cultivate relationships with those around him, whether they are with friends, family, or lovers. It's not difficult to feel sorry for Igby when we consider the craziness of his family. Everyone is combative and self-absorbed, hard hearted in their pursuit of power and money.

Igby, however, is not always a sympathetic character. He and Sookie spend much of their time patronizing other people and various philosophies. They act superior so they don't have to reflect on their own insecurities and inadequacies. Igby is guilty of running away from his problems, as well as creating some of his own. He certainly doesn't help himself when he runs away to Chicago to hang out in a hotel room courtesy of his mother's credit card. Or when he flees from the limo driver who's supposed to drive him to the airport so he can attend yet another new prep school.

Igby's mother, who is battling breast cancer, shrugs off his animosity as teen angst. She views her son as selfish and ungrateful, which is true to a certain point. But she does nothing to repair their broken relationship. Igby might act unfeeling and strong when he is in survival mode, but throughout the film he also demonstrates a caring attitude, especially toward Sookie and Rachel. Moments like these show the warmth Igby could reveal if given the opportunity to interact with selfless people whose behavior toward him was nurturing instead of destructive.

Despite the depressing drama, the film is smart and funny. It uses black comedy to comment on realistic issues and conflicts. The characters are quirky and the dialogue is razor sharp. Igby Slocumb is both a tragic and comic character, wisecracking his way through life while fearing he will end up like his father. At one point, Sookie looks him in the eye and says, "You're a furious boy. Eventually, you won't be a boy and it'll eat you up." As the story unfolds, the audience shares those same concerns. It soon becomes apparent that if Igby wants a better life, then he must leave home to find it.

Why You Should See This Film: Because it's about a snotty and defiant antihero who revolts against his narcissistic family.

Main Themes: Rebelliousness * Selfishness * Anger * Survival * Class

Classic Line: "Good things come to obsessive-compulsives who fixate."

Recommended Double Feature: *The Squid and the Whale* (2005); Rated R, 88 minutes, Drama-comedy

IT: CHAPTER ONE
(2017)

Directed by: Andy Muschietti
Written by: Chase Palmer, Cary Fukunaga, and Gary Dauberman, based on the novel *It* by Stephen King
Cast: Bill Skarsgard (Pennywise), Sophia Lillis (Beverly), Chosen Jacobs (Mike), Jack Dylan Grazer (Eddie), Jaeden Lieberher (Bill), Jackson Robert Scott (Georgie)
Rating: Rated R for violence, adult content, and adult language
Runtime: 135 minutes
Genre: Horror

The Gist: The film takes place in the town of Derry, Maine, where every twenty-seven years there is a rash of child disappearances. These vanishings are the result of a supernatural creature that takes the form of a creepy clown named Pennywise. The film centers on seven children that call themselves "The Losers Club." They must band together to defeat the evil entity that lurks in the sewers. While *It: Chapter One* is certainly a horror film, it is also a coming-of-age film that shows a loss of innocence and the power of friendship. As the children battle Pennywise, they must also deal with their own personal conflicts.

As the film opens in October 1988, Bill makes a sailboat for his seven-year-old brother, Georgie, who takes it outside in the rain so he can watch it float down the street. However, his sailboat falls down a storm drain. As he leans forward to retrieve it, he discovers Pennywise hiding in the sewer, holding the sailboat and asking Georgie if he wants it back. Their ensuing conversation is innocent enough, but as Georgie creeps closer to retrieve his sailboat the tone becomes unsettling and scary. Pennywise is terrifying because he can be charming and inviting one moment and then bloodthirsty and murderous the next.

Georgie's murder sets the stage for the rest of the film, which takes place during the summer of 1989. There are posters of missing children taped to telephone poles, reminding us that children are disappearing at an alarming rate. Bill, still distraught over Georgie, refuses to believe that his brother is dead. He takes it upon himself to search for clues as to where Georgie might be. In the midst of all this trauma, each of the seven kids begins to have strange and horrifying visions: a disturbing painting in a church seems to come to life; burning hands reach out in the darkness; strange voices rise up from a drain in the bathroom sink. As Pennywise reveals himself to the children in many shocking forms, they realize that they must face "it" if they want to survive.

First and foremost, *It* is a horror film. The scenes in the sewers are well constructed, creating a tense and claustrophobic atmosphere with

Jack Dylan Grazer, Jaeden Lieberher, Chosen Jacobs, Wyatt Oleff, Sophia Lillis, Jeremy Ray Taylor, Finn Wolfhard. ***Warner Bros./Photofest © Warner Bros.***

cavernous passageways and a minimal use of lighting. And some of the most unsettling scenes occur in a spooky house that is decrepit and full of ominous spaces. The film reminds us that there are really no safe spaces. What is especially unnerving is when Pennywise reveals himself in places not normally associated with horror, such as inside a church or a public library, or even in the middle of the street during a sunny day.

Because the novel is over one thousand pages in length, there are many subplots in the film. Eddie is a sickly child who is always carting around medicine and taking pills; he is happiest when he is hanging out with his friends and away from his overprotective mother. Beverly lives with her father, and it's clear from their relationship that he abuses her both physically and emotionally. And Mike is still reeling from the death of his parents in a house fire. Each of these kids, and others in the "Losers Club," harbor their own horrors, which they must overcome to defeat Pennywise.

The numerous subplots—which are not as fleshed out as they are in the novel—allow us to get to know the characters on a more personal level. When the characters are placed in dangerous situations, we become scared and more invested in the story. We like these kids, and we want them to succeed. They joke and fight with each other. They ride their bikes through small-town neighborhoods and try to avoid bullies. The boys have a crush on Beverly, and their flirtations with her are comical yet realistic in their sweetness and honesty.

These scenes offer a realistic depiction of childhood, which is carefree and innocent yet also cruel and confusing. The friends make fun of each other, yet they tend to each other when one of them becomes scared or injured. And it becomes clearer as the film progresses that the horrors these children experience definitely reflect—on a deeper and more graphic level—the challenges of moving from childhood into adolescence.

Pennywise preys on children because they are weak and vulnerable. They are trusting and naïve. The "Losers Club" needs to understand that it is natural to be afraid, but they cannot let fear rule them. And they cannot run away from Pennywise because to do so would be to avoid the problem rather than to confront it. Beverly tells the boys, "I want to run toward something, not away," and this poignant remark symbolizes the hopes and dreams that these kids possess. They might be young and inexperienced, but defeating Pennywise is their first step toward maturity.

Why You Should See This Film: Because it's a chilling tale that pits a supernatural evil against a group of gutsy children.

Main Themes: Bullying * Teamwork * Grief * Fear * Innocence

Classic Line: "When you're a kid, you think that you'll always be protected and cared for. Then, one day, you realize that's not true."

Recommended Double Feature: *Super 8* (2011); Rated PG-13, 112 minutes, Drama-fantasy

JUNO
(2007)

Directed by: Jason Reitman
Written by: Diablo Cody
Cast: Ellen Page (Juno), Michael Cera (Bleeker), Jennifer Garner (Vanessa), Jason Bateman (Mark), Allison Janney (Bren), J. K. Simmons (Mac), Olivia Thirlby (Leah)
Rating: Rated PG-13 for adult content, adult language, and mild violence
Runtime: 96 minutes
Genre: Comedy-drama

The Gist: Juno MacGuff is a sixteen-year-old junior with a laid-back attitude and great sense of humor. She likes to crack jokes, and she isn't afraid to speak her mind. Her bedroom is decorated with retro art and posters, and she talks with her friends on a hamburger phone. Juno has a stable home life with a supporting family. Her dad (Mac) is an HVAC repairman; her stepmother (Bren) is obsessed with dogs and owns a nail salon. Then there's her best friend, Leah, who has a crush on a middle-aged teacher at their high school.

One night, Juno has sex with Paulie Bleeker, one of her closest friends. Bleeker runs cross-country, is a bit shy, and constantly chews on orange Tic Tacs. Having drunk her weight in Sunny Delight and peed on several pregnancy test sticks, Juno accepts that she's pregnant and decides to schedule an abortion. While filling out the forms in the waiting room, however, she has a change of heart and decides to have the baby. The topic of abortion is a divisive issue, but the film does not dwell on Juno's time at the clinic. There is no graphic imagery or shouting protestors. In fact, the film doesn't offer a strong case either way for pro or con. Instead, it offers the termination of her pregnancy as simply an option that she considers.

Juno decides to give the baby up for adoption. After carefully perusing the penny saver, she discovers a cute married couple named Mark and Vanessa who want to adopt because they can't have children of their own. Vanessa can't wait to be a mother, and she obsesses over which color of yellow to paint the baby's room. Mark, however, has his own hesitations because there are several things he still wants to do with his life before he settles down to be a father. Mark and Vanessa are crucial characters because they reveal to Juno some of the difficulties in maintaining an adult relationship, as well as the importance of using effective communication.

Of course, Juno stresses over telling her parents that she's going to have a baby. But Mac and Bren are remarkably calm when Juno shares the news. Bren insists on buying her some prenatal vitamins, and her father seems more surprised that she slept with Paulie Bleeker. When Mac expresses his disappointment in Juno, she looks ashamed and tells him she's not really sure who she is. Her answer is regretful and honest, but also realistic. Like most young adults, she is trying to find her self-identity. The various relationships she has throughout the film—whether with her peers or with adults—will help her to figure out who she is and who she wants to be. Though Juno's parents don't scream and ground her for eternity, they are upset by the news. But they also understand the need to be supportive over the next nine months.

The rest of the film follows the hilarious, heartfelt, and quirky life of Juno as she struggles with adapting to her pregnancy and maintaining some semblance of a friendship with Bleeker, one that always seems on the verge of blossoming into a full-blown romance. Bleeker is clearly enamored with Juno, but she acts like she doesn't care. She only becomes jealous when he shows interest in another girl. The soundtrack, which is composed of indie rock songs, creates a folksy and whimsical atmosphere that helps to balance the film's mixture of humor and pathos while reflecting Juno's and Bleeker's easygoing attitudes.

In many ways, the film is about adult relationships, which Juno doesn't quite understand. Her numerous encounters with adult characters force her to wonder if two people can ever truly be happy. Such poignant moments, interspersed with the comedy, illustrate Juno's desire to explore beyond her boundaries. They also reveal her optimism, as well as her hope that despite all the hardships she's experiencing, the future will be sunny with blue skies.

Likewise, there are moments in the film when adults view her as eccentric. Her parents, while they love her, are not shy about calling out some of her immature decisions. Even Mark and Vanessa are unsure how to respond when they meet Juno for the first time and she cracks some jokes. Yes, Juno is unusual, but different can also mean unique. She is witty and sarcastic, and she excels at being her own person. She doesn't conform to what everyone else around her is saying or doing.

The film presents Juno's physical and emotional journey as integral to her growth and development. It also promotes positive family values like love and honesty. Juno herself understands the importance of those closest to her when she remarks, "I never realize how much I like being home unless I've been somewhere really different for a while." What makes the film so special is that the majority of the conflicts are a direct result of Juno's actions, and no matter where she is—whether at her parents' house, or at school, or visiting Mark and Vanessa—she is held accountable and must deal with them on her own.

Why You Should See This Film: Because it's a hilarious story of a smart and precocious young woman who wisecracks her way through bourgeoning romance and teen pregnancy.

Main Themes: Responsibility * Naïveté * Rebelliousness * Individuality * Judgment

Classic Line: "Somebody else is going to find a precious blessing from Jesus in this garbage dump of a situation."

Recommended Double Feature: *The Wackness* (2008); Rated R, 110 minutes, Drama-comedy

LADY BIRD
(2017)

Directed by: Greta Gerwig
Written by: Greta Gerwig
Cast: Saoirse Ronan (Lady Bird), Laurie Metcalf (Marion), Tracy Letts (Larry), Lucas Hedges (Danny), Beanie Feldstein (Julie), Timothée Chalamet (Kyle)
Rating: Rated R for language, sexual content, and drug use
Runtime: 95 minutes
Genre: Comedy-drama

The Gist: Like the best coming-of-age films, *Lady Bird*, which teeters between hilarity and sadness, explores conflicts between teenagers and their parents. It also highlights the adolescent desire to escape what's stable and secure at home so he or she can enjoy a more independent life. The film is raw and honest in its vivid portrayal of seventeen-year-old Christine McPherson. She's a student at a Catholic high school, and she's not particularly enamored with either her teachers or the other students. She also dislikes her hometown of Sacramento, which she describes as "soul killing."

Christine prefers to be called "Lady Bird" by everyone, including her family. She lives with her parents, her older brother, and her brother's girlfriend. Her family struggles financially, and it's clear Lady Bird is embarrassed that her family doesn't have a lot of money. She also fights constantly with her mother and feels disrespected at home. In giving herself the name Lady Bird, she asserts her desire to fly away. She believes that living with her family is stifling her growth and creativity.

The opening shot reveals Lady Bird and her mother lying on a bed. They face each other as they sleep. It is Lady Bird's senior year of high school, and the two of them are on a road trip to visit college campuses. This is an important image in the film because it suggests a strong mother and daughter relationship. As the film unfolds, it's obvious that Lady Bird and her mother are close, but their closeness also causes them to butt heads frequently. As an example, the very next scene shows them riding in a car, crying together as they listen to *The Grapes of Wrath* on audio. However, they quickly begin to argue and yell until Lady Bird throws herself from the car in a dramatic fit of rage. While this mood change is sudden and uncomfortable, it suggests the resentment and embarrassment that intensify between mother and daughter when Lady Bird decides to apply to colleges on the East Coast.

Lady Bird's decisions, both the good and the bad, show a young woman who makes bold choices to expand her horizons. She wants to

Saoirse Ronan, Laurie Metcalf. *A24/Photofest* © *A24*

prove she is independent enough to live by herself in New York City because her mother doesn't believe she's mature enough to survive on her own. Feeling emboldened by the lure of college, Lady Bird joins the theater program at her school and develops a crush on a boy named Danny. She drifts apart from her best friend, Julie, and starts hanging out with richer students who live the type of glamorous life she craves.

Lady Bird is bored with her life. She believes she can't succeed unless she leaves Sacramento. She also wants a boyfriend, which she thinks is the next big step in becoming an adult. However, her attempts to find love are funny and awkward. During one poignant moment of self-reflection, Lady Bird says, "I just had a whole experience that was wrong." It's one of the most honest scenes in the film because it reminds us that adolescence is sometimes filled with moments we expect to be fantastic and life changing, but which turn out to be unpleasant and disappointing.

Lady Bird has a strong relationship with her father, and he is supportive when she tells him she wants to attend college on the East Coast. Even though he's unemployed, he still helps her with the financial aid forms. He figures out how the family can help to pay her tuition. Her perseverance and excitement illustrate just how badly she wants to leave Sacramento, which is also realistic in that many adolescents experience a love/hate relationship with their hometown.

Though Lady Bird and her mother fight often, her mother is not mean or abusive. On the contrary, several scenes in the film reveal that her mother cares deeply about other people. In fact she wants nothing more than for her daughter to excel, telling her, "I want you to be the very best version of yourself that you can be." In between all of the bickering, Lady Bird and her mother enjoy going to open houses and dreaming about a better life. They shop for clothes together and share heartfelt conversations.

Lady Bird's journey throughout the film is an earnest attempt to discover just exactly who she is and who she can become. This involves dealing with family issues, discovering intimate relationships, and landing a job at a coffee shop where she falls for Kyle, a popular musician. The film is funny, heartrending, and enlightening, but always positive in affirming her growing maturity and independence. It also reminds us that the world can be uplifting one moment and then absolutely mortifying the next.

Why You Should See This Film: Because it's an awkward and humorous snapshot of a turbulent senior year laden with friendship drama and family crises.

Main Themes: Communication * Family * Rebelliousness * Sexual Discovery * Anger

Classic Line: "Being successful doesn't mean anything in and of itself. It just means that you're successful. But that doesn't mean that you're happy."

Recommended Double Feature: *Boyhood* (2014); Rated R, 166 minutes, Drama

THE LAST PICTURE SHOW
(1971)

Directed by: Peter Bogdanovich
Written by: Larry McMurtry and Peter Bogdanovich, based on the novel by Larry McMurtry
Cast: Jeff Bridges (Duane), Cybil Shepherd (Jacy), Cloris Leachman (Ruth), Ben Johnson (Sam), Timothy Bottoms (Sonny), Ellen Burstyn (Lois), Sam Bottoms (Billy), Eileen Brennan (Genevieve)
Rating: Rated R for nudity, sexuality, and language
Runtime: 118 minutes
Genre: Drama

The Gist: Often considered one of the most important films of the 1970s, *The Last Picture Show* explores life in 1951 in the town of Anarene, Texas, near Wichita Falls. It presents a mosaic of well-developed characters, composed of adults and adolescents. Over the course of the film, they argue and reconcile, fall in and out of love, and struggle with whether to remain in Anarene or to leave it in search of something better.

Anarene appears desolate and on the decline, a dusty place full of boredom and simmering resentment. The beginning of the film takes place in a pool hall owned by Sam the Lion. He's a fatherly figure who recognizes the value in the teenagers who frequent his pool hall and movie theater. He talks with Sonny and Duane, two best friends who play on the high school football team. Sam chides them for not winning the game and asks them if they have any school spirit. Sonny responds that he doesn't know, and his apathetic delivery is emblematic of the attitude exhibited by most of his friends. They've been drained of their spirit by living in a place that's becoming a ghost town.

Duane is dating Jacy, the most beautiful girl in town. She uses the men around her for selfish reasons. She hopes to land someone who has money and power, and who can offer her a more glamorous life. She strategizes how she can use them to endure the monotony of Anarene. But despite the boredom, Jacy doesn't want to leave her hometown, even when her mother (Lois) tells her that everything is flat and empty. Lois fears that Jacy will make the same mistakes she once made. As well, her mother's bluntness echoes the sentiment of the other characters. In Anarene, there's nothing to do except reminisce about the good days or regret poor decisions.

Sonny begins an affair with Ruth, an older woman who's the wife of the basketball coach. He is also friends with Billy, a mute boy under Sam's care. The scenes between Billy and Sonny are poignant, especially in a film that lacks the strong presence of father figures. Then there's Genevieve, the waitress who works at the café and takes a genuine interest in the lives of her customers. The secondary characters in the film are important because they help to develop the main characters. For example, a wealthy boy is attracted to Jacy, but he doesn't want to have sex with her because she's a virgin, so he tells her to come back after she's slept with someone. This short conversation, which might seem insignificant, has lasting implications for several of the main characters.

The Last Picture Show was shot in black and white, which creates an older look that clearly sets the story in the past between World War II and the Korean War. The grittiness and lack of color contribute to the demoralized mood and enhance the oppressive atmosphere in which these characters strive to find some meaning in their lives. The film depicts the frustrations experienced by adolescents who are fumbling their way through sexual situations while yearning to escape from the constrictions of small-town life. In one way or another, the characters are selfish. And it's not always because they're mean and self-centered, but because being selfish helps them to survive in Anarene. Pursuing their own self-interests at the expense of others seems to be the only way they can cling to hope and keep alive their dreams for a better life.

Even the adults, who struggle with their own troubled relationships, are an important part of the film. They show what might happen to these teenagers if they decide to follow the same paths as their parents. As well, it's interesting to examine how the two generations interact and view one another. Sam the Lion talks with Sonny about a woman he once loved with heartbreaking honesty. Later, Sonny chats with Genevieve about his love life, complaining that the only pretty girl in town is Jacy, but since Duane is dating her, she's off limits. Genevieve's response—"Jacy will bring him more misery than she'll ever be worth"—is a reminder that attractiveness and popularity are not the defining aspects of a relationship. The biggest problem for these characters is that they don't know how to communicate with each other. Throughout the film, it's a lack of understanding that leads to breakups, acts of rebellion, impromptu marriages, and violent fights.

The Last Picture Show is a film about fractured relationships, raw in its portrayal of anger and jealousy. By observing these characters—by celebrating their smart decisions and suffering with them through the bad ones—we can understand more deeply the importance of Anarene's emptiness and how the landscape impacts not only their attitudes, but also their self-identities.

Why You Should See This Film: Because it's a rich character study about the intersecting lives of adolescents in a small Texas town that has seen better days.

Main Themes: Disillusionment * Guilt * Sexual Discovery * Naïveté * Apathy

Classic Line: "Being crazy about a woman like her is always the right thing to do. Being an old decrepit bag of bones, that's what's ridiculous. Gettin' old."

Recommended Double Feature: *The Man in the Moon* (1991); Rated PG-13, 100 minutes, Drama

LOVE, SIMON
(2018)

Directed by: Greg Berlanti
Written by: Elizabeth Berger and Isaac Aptaker, based on the novel *Simon vs. the Homo Sapiens Agenda* by Becky Albertalli
Cast: Nick Robinson (Simon), Jennifer Garner (Emily), Josh Duhamel (Jack), Katherine Langford (Leah), Alexandra Shipp (Abby), Jorge Lendeborg Jr. (Nick), Logan Miller (Martin)
Rating: Rated PG-13 for thematic elements, sexual references, language, and teen partying
Runtime: 110 minutes
Genre: Romantic comedy–drama

The Gist: Here is a touching comment on the struggles of self-identity and sharing one's sexuality. This film centers on a senior named Simon who is gay and yearns to come out to his friends and family. The film deals with not only his personal struggles, but how those struggles affect his relationships with everyone around him. This is an uplifting and inspirational story that teaches us the importance of being true to yourself and of fighting for what you believe in.

The film is narrated by Simon, whose voice-over is warm and engaging. The opening scenes show him interacting with his family. He receives a car as a gift and tells viewers that his life is normal. Except Simon has a secret. And it's not until he reads an online post from an anonymous gay student, also grappling with his sexuality, that Simon wrestles with who to tell he is gay and how he should tell them. As Simon and the anonymous student—who identifies himself as Blue—begin a heartfelt correspondence via email, several conflicts arise that force the characters to communicate more openly and to be honest in their true feelings for each other.

The characters in *Love, Simon* talk like real people, not like one-dimensional characters who speak merely to move the plot along. These are characters who care about each other and enjoy spending time together. Anyone who feels comfortable hanging out with a specific group of people can relate to the comradery shared among Simon, Leah, Abby, and Nick. They're typical high school students, which helps us to empathize with them. However, in addition to Simon's secret, there are other conflicts within their tight-knit group, specifically the fact that Nick likes Abby. He keeps stressing out over whether he should ask her out.

One day in the library, Simon forgets to sign out of his email account. Another student (Martin) reads and screenshots all of the emails between Simon and Blue, then blackmails Simon into helping him win Abby's heart. His blackmail is not based on hatred or revenge, but on selfishness. In this age of Snapchat and Instagram, one of the film's powerful lessons

Nick Robinson, Clark Moore. *Twentieth Century Fox/Photofest © Twentieth Century Fox*

is to be careful when using social media, a trap many teenagers have fallen into. Technology can be awesome and make our lives easier, but it can also violate our privacy and ruin important relationships. Still, despite the anger and stress brought about by Martin's possession of the emails, the ensuing drama does force Simon to be more introspective. He learns how his actions affect others, and he realizes the importance of being an individual during a time in his life when so many people are constantly trying to be just like everyone else.

Unlike many coming-of-age films, *Love, Simon* creates a world in which the main character is nurtured and supported at home. There are no ugly fights with parents and siblings, no one running out of the house and screaming that he or she is misunderstood. Simon likes spending time with his younger sister, and his parents are hip and fun. They respect his independence while still guiding and encouraging him. There are several scenes where the entire family spends time together, whether eating a meal or watching a movie. During these moments, it's clear how Simon's positive home life has affected how he treats others and how he wants to be treated himself.

While many films divide their characters into social groups, *Love, Simon* allows its characters the opportunity to mix together. Abby and Simon are acting in the school play, but Nick plays on the soccer team. These friends are not joined together by clichés, but by deeper bonds that allow them to share an honesty not often seen in coming-of-age films. They talk openly about sex and parents and relationships. Their humorous, yet candid, exchanges draw us closer into the film because they reveal characters who have fears and wonders and uncertainties, much like ourselves.

The main characters in the film are not mean and nasty. Some of them make poor choices and have to learn from their mistakes. Their bad decisions alienate them at a time when having close friends is a crucial part of their growth and development. At one point, Leah tells Simon, "Sometimes, I feel like I'm always on the outside," and he understands exactly what she means, not just because he has been hiding his homosexuality, but because he has fallen in love with Blue and still doesn't know his true identity.

An important message is that everyone has issues. Everyone feels like an outcast at certain times, but it's how we deal with those tough challenges that helps to define us. In one poignant scene, Simon sits by himself in a Ferris wheel, looking out at the world, and we're reminded that our lives are always in motion. Sometimes we are up and sometimes we are down, but we should always be striving to move forward.

Why You Should See This Film: Because it's a feel-good story about battling prejudice to find love.

Main Themes: Fear * Courage * Deception * Prejudice * Communication

Classic Line: "Announcing who you are to the world is pretty terrifying because what if the world doesn't like you?"

Recommended Double Feature: *The Miseducation of Cameron Post* (2018); Not Rated, 96 minutes, Drama-romance

LUCAS
(1986)

Directed by: David Seltzer
Written by: David Seltzer
Cast: Corey Haim (Lucas), Kerri Green (Maggie), Charlie Sheen (Cappie), Winona Ryder (Rina), Courtney Thorne-Smith (Alise)
Rating: Rated PG-13 for adult language
Runtime: 100 minutes
Genre: Comedy-drama-romance

The Gist: Lucas Bly is a fourteen-year-old nerd who wears large glasses and lives a secluded life with few friends. He's an accelerated student who listens to classical music and likes to use big words like "superficial" and "materialism." His intelligence is the only power he can wield over his classmates. His father, never seen in the film, is an alcoholic, and this embarrassment causes Lucas to lie about where he lives and what his father does for a living. When frustrated or sad, Lucas hides underneath a bridge by the railroad tracks where he can be alone with his thoughts.

Small for his age, Lucas is ignored and bullied in equal measures. He wanders the railroad tracks examining insects because he finds them fascinating. The opening shot shows Lucas watching a cicada emerge from its cocoon, and it's clear—given his intense concentration—that he relates to its innocence and vulnerability. Rather than collect the insects, he studies them and comments on their beauty. Lucas is an observer, always existing on the periphery and not really belonging to any specific group.

But when he falls in love with sixteen-year-old Maggie, who has recently moved to town, his world is turned upside down. When they first meet, she is playing tennis while Lucas watches her from the other side of the fence. As he watches her, he plays classical music on a tape recorder in his backpack, elevating an ordinary, everyday moment to a romantic one as he watches Maggie's hair twirl around as she leaps in the air and swings her racket at the tennis ball. Despite his odd behavior and his unique perspective on life, Maggie finds Lucas interesting and funny. Throughout the film, their conversations are not shallow and self-serving, but rich and contemplative.

Lucas's plans to date Maggie are complicated by several other relationships that develop over the course of the film. A fellow classmate named Rina likes Lucas, but he is both oblivious and indifferent to her attention; Maggie likes Cappie, a football player who befriends and protects Lucas from the jocks that make fun of him; and then there is Alise, Cappie's girlfriend who notices and becomes jealous of Maggie and Cappie's flirtations. These characters are constantly jockeying for attention. But what's interesting is how they move among different cliques throughout the film, and how their personalities change as they do so.

His pushiness to spend time with Maggie is both awkward and tragic because we know she is only interested in him as a friend. Nevertheless, in a display of misguided determination, Lucas tells Cappie there's a school dance. Trying to play it cool, he suggests that he and Maggie double-date with Cappie and Alise. His argument is that Maggie needs to meet new people because she has a strong need for acceptance. These comments show how Lucas tries to compensate for his weaknesses by projecting them onto others so he can be heroic. He wants to be valued and respected, and he is searching for the opportunity to prove himself.

Lucas becomes upset when Maggie spends more time with Cappie, especially when Cappie convinces her to try out for the cheerleading team. And when Lucas tries to deter her from joining the team by ridiculing it, Maggie becomes defensive and says, "Just because you don't approve of something doesn't mean other people don't have a right to enjoy it." Her point is that we all have different passions or fears or desires. Friends should champion each other's differences, not mock them. Lucas is being judgmental because he wants to date Maggie. He knows he can't compete with Cappie, who is handsome and popular. In trying to build a more intimate friendship, though, Lucas alienates Maggie with his condescending remarks.

Toward the end of the film, Lucas decides to try out for the football team. He wants to silence those who make fun of him and call him names like "leukoplakia." His unwavering tenacity to be a part of the team is admirable and funny, but it also provides some of the film's more dramatic moments. The film is honest in its portrayal of teenagers, not just in how they act, but in how they talk. They have intelligent conversations and they aren't afraid to share their hopes and dreams. The screenplay allows them to wonder, and it doesn't fault them for it. Instead, the characters' thoughts and questions are regarded as a natural part of growing up.

Lucas succeeds as a coming-of-age film precisely because it addresses important ideas like tolerance and compassion, as well as the basic human desire to feel included. In one of the film's most effective and moving scenes, the characters are assembled on a stage for choir practice. The camera slowly moves from character to character as Rina looks at Lucas, who is looking at Maggie, who is looking at Cappie, who is being watched by Alise. In high school, everyone is always concerned with what everyone else is doing. More importantly, they are always concerned with why they are doing it.

Why You Should See This Film: Because it's a sweet and uplifting story of a lonely teen who experiences love and heartbreak for the first time.

Main Themes: Bullying * Friendship * Jealousy * Perseverance * Acceptance

Classic Line: "There are certain people you like in a certain way and others you like as a friend. I don't know why."

Recommended Double Feature: *Angus* (1995); Rated PG-13, 90 minutes, Comedy-drama

ME AND EARL AND THE DYING GIRL

(2015)

Directed by: Alfonso Gomez-Rejon
Written by: Jesse Andrews, based on the novel by Jesse Andrews
Cast: Thomas Mann (Greg), RJ Cyler (Earl), Olivia Cooke (Rachel), Connie Britton (Mom)
Rating: Rated PG-13 for adult content and adult language
Runtime: 105 minutes
Genre: Drama-comedy

The Gist: This funny and touching story focuses on Greg Gaines, a lanky and awkward senior at Schenley High School who drifts through his high school years without forming any strong relationships. He hates referring to people as "friends." As a result, he is on pleasant terms with everyone, but he has few buddies. Because Greg refuses to belong to a socially accepted group, he eats lunch in his history teacher's office with Earl, the closest thing he has to a best friend. Earl is a fellow student whom Greg refers to as a coworker because they make crappy movies together as a hobby.

At the beginning of the film, sitting in front of his computer, Greg admits to the viewer that he is unsure how to tell this story. His inability to communicate—as well as his hesitation to share his feelings with other people—reflects his self-imposed isolation and lack of empathy. Nevertheless, Greg is not shy about stating that fact that the story he will relate is about his senior year of high school and how it destroyed his life. The rest of the story explores the developing friendship among the three main characters who are referenced in the film's title, namely, Greg, Earl, and a classmate named Rachel.

Greg's life changes when his mother forces him to spend time with Rachel, who recently discovered she has leukemia. When he arrives at Rachel's house, she tells him she doesn't want to hang out. They aren't friends, and she refuses to accept any pity. It's only when Greg explains that he doesn't want his mom hounding him—and that Rachel would actually be doing him a favor—that she allows him into her room. Despite his lack of social skills, and his anger at being forced to go to her house, the two of them become friends.

Rachel and Greg find it easy to talk with each other. Their conversations are poignant and funny, revealing fears and truths about the kind of people they are, like when Greg tells her he is awkward and has a face like a groundhog. Or when Rachel confesses how upset she is that their classmates act so different around her because they know she is sick. She finds their behavior insulting and wants to tell them that they're not helping. Here are two characters who both need each other at this crucial time in their lives. Greg has to learn to fit in and talk to people on a personal

Olivia Cooke, Thomas Mann, RJ Cyler. ***Fox Searchlight Pictures/Photofest © Fox Searchlight Pictures***

level, while Rachel needs to feel included because of her cancer and the subsequent chemotherapy.

In the midst of their blossoming friendship, Earl and Greg continue to make homemade movies. They both enjoy classic films, including foreign ones, so they watch them often at Greg's house, which is artsy and full of books. Greg says that he and Earl like watching those movies because they are "weird and often violent, like us. Or confusing and possibly meaningless, like life." It's clear that watching and making films is an outlet for Greg to express himself. It also provides him with a social opportunity to hang out with Earl. Together, they remake many of the films they watch. They create short films and give them ridiculous titles like *Senior Citizen Cane*, *Eyes Wide Butt*, and *Brew Velvet*.

One day, someone asks Greg to make one of his homemade movies for Rachel. Despite being uncomfortable with the request, he agrees. For months, he struggles to make the movie. When he continues to complain about the pressure, Earl becomes angry and accuses him of treating Rachel like a burden and of not understanding the magnitude of her situation. Since Greg is a person who hides his feelings and tries to be invisible, it's difficult for him to admit that he's concerned about Rachel's health or that he's worried about her.

Eventually, he and Earl decide to interview Rachel's friends and classmates. It's clear that Greg wants to make a special movie for his friend, but he doesn't know how to make something that is expressive and significant. His process of trying to make sense of this special project—of developing a particular method and brainstorming ideas—parallels his own emotional journey throughout the film as he develops self-confidence. Greg learns to become active rather than passive, though he doesn't always achieve the best results. For example, he tries to fit in while having lunch in the cafeteria, but he panics and botches the attempt, thereby disrupting his plan to be as inconspicuous as possible.

Greg announces at the beginning of the film that he is not sharing a touching and romantic story. In many ways, the film plays with clichés and challenges our expectations. Yes, this is a film in which death and cancer play an important role in shaping the characters and events, but the story is refreshing in the way it constantly surprises us. It's sad and funny and insightful, often in the same scene. And in presenting us with dark themes from which most of us would rather shy away, the film shows how we can embrace those conflicts so as to enrich our own lives.

———

Why You Should See This Film: Because it presents an offbeat friendship between an insecure high school student and a tough-minded classmate who's battling cancer.

Main Themes: Apathy * Death * Ambition * Self-Confidence * Acceptance

Classic Line: "One last thing. Hot girls destroy your life. That's just a fact. It doesn't matter if the hot girl is also a good person."

Recommended Double Feature: *The Fundamentals of Caring* (2016); Rated TV-MA, 93 minutes, Drama-comedy

MEAN GIRLS

(2004)

Directed by: Mark Waters

Written by: Tina Fey, based on the novel *Queen Bees and Wannabes* by Rosalind Wiseman

Cast: Lindsay Lohan (Cady), Rachel McAdams (Regina), Lacey Chabert (Gretchen), Amanda Seyfried (Karen), Lizzy Caplan (Janis), Jonathan Bennett (Aaron), Daniel Franzese (Damian)

Rating: Rated PG-13 for sexual content, language, and some teen partying

Runtime: 97 minutes

Genre: Comedy

The Gist: Hilarious and satirical, this film shows the damaging effects of cliques in high schools. Cady is sixteen years old and beginning her first year of public school. She's been homeschooled her entire life because both of her parents are research zoologists. For the past twelve years, her family has lived in Africa. Despite Cady's optimism, her first day of school is stressful and chaotic. She doesn't understand the rules and regulations. She gets into trouble for trying to go to the bathroom without a lavatory pass. Her teachers yell at her for bringing food to class. And she is chastised for using a green pen.

For Cady, it's strange to be in a place where adults don't trust her, as well as a place where students are so concerned with social status. Rather than study material in their classes, most of the students study each other. Because Cady has never attended public school, she hasn't been programmed to worry about what she is wearing or what new slang term she's using in the cafeteria. Therefore, it's interesting to witness the high school experience from the perspective of an outsider. Cady tells people her parents sent her to public school so she would become socialized, but she soon learns that high school has its own set of rules and expectations.

On her first day of school, ignored by everyone, she eats lunch in one of the bathroom stalls. Eventually, she befriends two other students, Janis and Damian. Damian is gay and Janis is a goth artist. Both of them are not popular, but they welcome Cady and help her feel included. They explain to her that the most famous group at school is known as "The Plastics." The group consists of three girls: Regina, Karen, and Gretchen. Regina is the ringleader, and she's referred to as the Queen Bee by the other students. Together, these three girls are the most beautiful and popular in the high school. They're considered teen royalty.

One day, the Plastics invite Cady to sit with them for lunch. She is surprised by all of their self-imposed rules. For example, they're not allowed to wear a tank top two days in a row, they can only wear their hair in a ponytail once a week, and they can only wear jeans or track pants on Fridays. The Plastics are glamorous, but they are also selfish and superficial. Gretchen sums up this idea best when she says, "I'm sorry that people are so jealous of me. But I can't help it that I'm popular." The Plastics are a manipulative and controlling group that thrives on status and acceptance. None of them can keep a secret, and they love to gossip. Each one of them takes pleasure in wielding power over the others. They are the very definition of mean girls.

Cady joins their group and learns that the Plastics have created a "Burn Book," which is basically a hateful scrapbook. They cut out yearbook pictures of other girls in their class, paste them onto the blank pages, and write crude comments. Cady is shocked at their spitefulness, which she observes both at and away from school. The time she spends with the Plastics helps her to understand the strange behavior of most adolescents. While at the mall, Cady says that being there reminds her of being in Africa. The students, much like the animals, are in heat and traveling in packs. This comparison occurs several times throughout the film. It highlights the negative effect of cliques in high schools. Instead of trying to develop their own self-identities, all the students mirror what their peers say and do. There is a social order, much like the animal kingdom, but instead of being established on strength, it's established on popularity. The film suggests that being part of a group is the only way to survive high school.

Cady spends more and more time with the Plastics, but complications ensue when she develops a crush on Aaron, who is Regina's ex-boyfriend. Regina offers to be a good friend and speak to Aaron, but then she sabotages the relationship. Infuriated, Cady conspires with Janis and Damian to get revenge on the Plastics. She turns them against each other, which is not difficult. Because the three girls are selfish, their friendship is built on paranoia and lies rather than on trust and honesty.

What's interesting is that while Cady dislikes Regina, she still wants the Queen Bee to like her. And the more Cady hangs out with the Plastics, the more she acts like them. The film illustrates how much adolescents crave attention and how important it is to be admired. Cady enjoys her newfound popularity, and she's surprised at how easy it is to control everyone around her. As the backstabbing escalates and the gossip runs rampant, the school erupts into chaos. The film shows that in high school there is no such thing as keeping secrets because telling a secret is way more exciting than keeping one.

Why You Should See This Film: Because it's a perceptive social commentary that explores the mentality of high school hierarchy.

Main Themes: Jealousy * Insecurity * Pretentiousness * Judgment * Conformity

Classic Line: "Irregardless, ex-boyfriends are just off limits to friends. I mean, that's just, like, the rules of feminism."

Recommended Double Feature: *The DUFF* (2015); Rated PG-13, 110 minutes, Romantic comedy

MOANA
(2016)

Directed by: Ron Clements, John Musker
Written by: Jared Bush
Cast: Auli'i Cravalho (Moana), Dwayne Johnson (Maui), Temuera Morrison (Chief Tui), Rachel House (Gramma Tala), Jemaine Clement (Tamatoa)
Rating: Rated PG for peril, some scary images, and brief thematic elements
Runtime: 107 minutes
Genre: Adventure-animation

The Gist: *Moana* is full of lush animation and catchy songs, but it's also an effective coming-of-age story that cares deeply about its characters and their search for meaning. During the opening moments, we are told that the demigod Maui stole the heart of Te Fiti and gave it to mankind so it would have the power of creation. That this action sends Maui into exile, gives rise to the villain Te Kā, and initiates a darkness that permeates the land is a strong sign that perhaps the power to create should not rest with mankind, but with nature. Indeed, one of the film's important messages is about respecting the natural world and appreciating all that it can provide. There is a balance—a symbiotic relationship—between nature and mankind that must be respected. When that balance is corrupted, chaos ensues.

Moana (voiced by Auli'i Cravalho), Maui (voiced by Dwayne Johnson). ***Walt Disney Studios/Photofest © Walt Disney Studios***

Moana is sixteen years old and lives on the island of Motu Nui in the Pacific Ocean. She is slated to become chief of her tribe. Like most teenagers, she yearns to travel past her village and to see the world for herself, a desire not embraced by her father. He continuously orders her not to go beyond the reef. He assures her that the village is all she needs. For a teenager who feels trapped living with her parents, the island is a great symbol for the isolation and frustration Moana feels.

These early scenes on the island are rich with young adult themes. Moana voices her creative ideas for how to save her tribe from a blight that has struck the island. But her father refuses to listen because he believes she is harboring childish notions. Then there is Moana's supportive grandmother who encourages her to listen to the voice inside of her. Moana's father appears overbearing and controlling, but he is not a mean person. He must learn to trust his daughter, just like Moana must learn to trust herself, and just like Maui must regain his self-confidence to believe he can defeat Te Kā.

Yes, Moana must embark on an important journey to save her homeland from a lava-spewing volcano monster with the help of a buff and arrogant demigod. But the physical journey she endures also parallels the emotional journey she must experience before she can return home and be an effective leader. Moana understands that she must leave the island, find Maui, and make him return Te Fiti's heart. For only then can Te Kā's darkness stop poisoning the island. Moana, however, does not yet realize the importance of the journey itself. She is focused on the destination, wanting the results without appreciating the process.

At one point, Maui asks Moana, "Why didn't the ocean take the heart back to Te Fiti itself, or bring me my hook?" The answer, of course, is clear: Moana was chosen by the ocean to undertake this voyage, and she must be the one to finish it. She must make decisions by herself, whether they are right or wrong. She must separate from her parents and survive on her own. Moana comes to know herself better during her lengthy time on the ocean, not just in learning how to sail, but in trusting her instincts and in grasping her own limitations. She wants to prove herself as a strong leader, but she needs to recognize when overconfidence leads to impulsiveness.

At its core, *Moana* is about searching for oneself. It's about understanding the important idea—as Moana eloquently states—that "sometimes, our strengths lie beneath the surface." And it's about not being able to appreciate where you're from until you travel somewhere else. The importance of teamwork is illustrated through the various relationships. For example, Moana's grandmother shows her a hidden cave full of ships, which sets her journey in motion. And if the ocean had not acted as a sidekick—leading Moana to Maui's island and continuously placing her back on the boat when he throws her overboard—then Moana might have perished at sea.

Finally, there is the relationship between Moana and Maui. At first, Maui questions the strengths and skills of a teenage girl. Yet, Moana saves him from Tamatoa, the greedy crab who holds Maui's fish hook. And when Maui realizes he has lost his power to shapeshift, it's Moana who builds up his self-confidence. Just like Moana needs Maui's help to save Motu Nui from the blight, Maui also needs Moana to reclaim his powers and atone for his past mistakes.

The richness of the film's themes are complemented by wonderful songs such as "How Far I'll Go," "You're Welcome," and "Shiny." These musical interludes are not merely fun transitions that lead us from one plot point to the next. Instead, they contribute to the narrative by developing the main characters. The lyrics and melodies reveal a character's particular strengths and weaknesses, or a character's fears and desires. They deepen the film's conflicts and contribute to the necessary mood of a specific scene, whether it is hope, arrogance, or vanity. In doing so, the songs help to humanize the characters. They draw us further into the story by allowing us to recognize pieces of ourselves inside each one of them.

Why You Should See This Film: Because it's a tropical blend of spunky determination and selfless heroism.

Main Themes: Courage * Leadership * Empowerment * Self-Awareness * Trust

Classic Line: "There comes a day when you're gonna look around and realize happiness is where you are."

Recommended Double Feature: *Kubo and the Two Strings* (2016); Rated PG, 102 minutes, Adventure-fantasy-animation

A MONSTER CALLS

(2016)

Directed by: J. A. Bayona
Written by: Patrick Ness, based on his novel
Cast: Lewis MacDougall (Conor), Sigourney Weaver (Grandma), Felicity Jones (Mum), James Melville (Harry), Liam Neeson (The Monster)
Rating: Rated PG-13 for mild violence and adult content
Runtime: 108 minutes
Genre: Drama-fantasy

The Gist: This emotional film is about a young boy named Conor who must deal with his mother's terminal illness. When the story begins, he is visited by a monster—in the form of a gigantic yew tree—that explains it will share three stories with him. At the conclusion of the third story, Conor must tell the Monster a fourth one. Each of these stories is a dark fairy tale that relates to Conor's life. The first involves a prince and a witch who battle over control of a kingdom. The second focuses on the clashes between a parson and an apothecary. And the third is about a man who is invisible and calls upon the Monster to help him because he wants people to notice him. The fourth concerns Conor himself and his inability to process his emotions.

While the film is live action, the Monster's stories are all animated. As a result, each story exudes a bleak and surreal quality that matches Conor's attitude. His moods—which range from denial and hopeful to angry and violent—reflect the normal behavior of someone experiencing death for the first time. The animation contains a lot of shadows and blurred colors that symbolize Conor's depression, as well as his confusion regarding how he should cope with his mother's illness. The themes and ideas presented in the Monster's stories are thought provoking and complex. They mirror the challenges and decisions that Conor himself must face, whether at school, at home, or at the hospital while visiting his mother.

The story begins, as the Monster says, "like so many stories. With a boy, too old to be a kid, too young to be a man." Conor is on the precipice of adolescence. He should be interested in girls and hanging out with friends. Instead, he worries about his mother and tries to maintain normalcy amid so much change. In addition, Conor is fighting with his grandmother and dealing with a trio of bullies at school. Part of his frustration is certainly his lack of control over his mother's debilitating illness. He wants to help her, but household chores and kind words can only do so much. He is learning that sometimes life can be unfair.

One of those forces is time. The Monster always arrives at 12:07—sometimes in the morning and sometimes in the afternoon—to share its stories. And it soon becomes apparent that 12:07 holds an important significance. Throughout the film, Conor wants to spend more time with his mother. He can feel the days and hours slipping away. He tries to be encouraging when the doctor prescribes new medication; his words seem forced and rehearsed, as if he is trying to convince himself of something he doesn't believe.

Another powerful force that Conor must endure is the bullying at school. Harry and two other boys taunt him on a daily basis. During

Liam Neeson (as the Monster), Lewis MacDougall. ***Focus Features/Photofest*** **©** ***Focus Features***

these fights, Conor refuses to retaliate, appearing indifferent to the abuse he receives. It's almost as if he welcomes the attention because the adults in his life are acting so strange around him. They appear more concerned and hesitant, which Conor hates because their behavior reminds him that his mother is dying. All Conor wants is to be treated like a regular kid.

Because the Monster is a yew tree, whose berries and bark possess healing powers used in various medicines, Conor believes the Monster can help save his mother. However, there are other people in the story who need to be saved. Conor himself must confront the truth of a recurring dream he's having; he must reconnect with his estranged dad who lives in America with a new family; and he must strengthen the relationship with his grandmother when his mother's condition worsens and he is forced to live with her.

Given that the words "yew" and "you" are homonyms, perhaps the Monster represents Conor's subconscious. If so, then the three stories might be Conor's attempt to better understand the actions of himself and others. Given how little control he has over events in his life, it makes sense that he would attempt to control his fears. In this way, the Monster's destructive behavior symbolizes Conor's rage. The towering presence of the Monster—with its booming voice and its strong branches—helps him to forget how helpless he is to save his mother.

At one point, the Monster tells Conor that it's not important what people think, but what they do. Conor can't hide his emotions forever. He can't pretend that his problems will turn out exactly the way he wants. The more Conor fights to keep his feelings inside, the more resentment builds up until he runs the risk of alienating everyone around him. At some point he must face the reality of his mother's situation. He must learn how to process his grief. Only then can Conor admit to himself how he feels, and only then can he begin to heal properly.

Why You Should See This Film: Because it's a sad and poignant story about the process of grief and the healing power of narrative.

Main Themes: Death * Anger * Guilt * Acceptance * Fear

Classic Line: "There is not always a good guy. Nor is there always a bad one. Most people are somewhere in between."

Recommended Double Feature: *Hugo* (2011); Rated PG, 129 minutes, Drama-fantasy

MONSTER HOUSE
(2006)

Directed by: Gil Kenan
Written by: Dan Harmon, Rob Schrab, and Pamela Pettler
Cast: Steve Buscemi (Mr. Nebbercracker), Mitchel Musso (DJ), Sam Lerner (Chowder), Spencer Locke (Jenny)
Rating: Rated PG for scary images and sequences, thematic elements, some crude humor, and brief language
Runtime: 91 minutes
Genre: Horror-fantasy-animation

The Gist: *Monster House* is an entertaining story centering on a trio of children who battle an angry, possessed house that eats trespassers. When the house, which is owned by the cantankerous Mr. Nebbercracker, comes alive with the spirit of his dead wife, the children must battle the house to save themselves and their neighborhood. With windows in place of eyes, and porch railings substituting for teeth, the monster house seems alive and menacing, even in the middle of a beautiful, sunny day. Bare, gnarled trees line the house on either side of the yard, and this creepy mood is intensified whenever Mr. Nebbercracker screams at the children who venture onto his property.

These strange actions are noticed by twelve-year-old DJ, the film's main character, who watches Mr. Nebbercracker through a telescope in his upstairs bedroom from across the street. His parents, however, ignore his incessant warnings about the monster house, interpreting his spying and observations as nothing more than pubescent whims. Yet, despite his insistence that he's too old to go trick-or-treating, or his desire to be spoken to like an adult, DJ still clings to childish traits. For example, he has a stuffed animal, a rabbit, which he keeps on his bed and which he clings to in moments of terror and confusion.

DJ hangs out with his best friend, Chowder. And when Chowder's basketball bounces into Nebbercracker's yard, he whines until DJ ventures toward the monster house to retrieve it. Chowder is clearly the more immature of the two characters, a point made obvious when Mr. Nebbercracker catches DJ on his lawn and drags him toward the monster house. Chowder, refusing to leave the safety of the sidewalk to help his friend, looks around the neighborhood and shouts for help. These two characters are important because they represent both sides of the pubertal coin. Chowder clings to childhood and its simplicity, wearing a red cape and making fart noises with his armpit, while DJ attempts to act more responsibly by thinking through his decisions and by risking his life to save others.

Jenny is a two-term class president at Westbrook Prep who roams the suburban streets to sell candy. The boys' first glimpse of her is through the telescope in DJ's bedroom, and the scene is played for laughs as they fight for control of it so they can gaze upon her beauty. Later, as they both try to impress her, it becomes clear that these boys are developing an avid interest in girls and are trying their hardest not to appear childish and immature. Anyone who has ever tried to impress someone can relate to the awkwardness of these humorous scenes, as well as to the realization that the more DJ and Chowder try to act older, the younger they actually appear until their actions become embarrassing rather than charming.

But when Mr. Nebbercracker collapses on his front lawn from an apparent heart attack, the monster house suddenly roars to life with a vengeance and the three characters must join together to defeat it. The monster house itself is a marvel of set design and animation, especially when it transforms from a rickety old house into a manifestation of Mr. Nebbercracker's wife, slamming shut its front door, erupting long flames from the fireplace, and billowing thick, black smoke out of the chimney. The scenes involving the monster house are some of the most energetic in the film, combining action, comedy, and suspense as the characters are forced to work together and brainstorm creative ideas while the house rises up from its foundation to go on a rampage through the neighborhood.

In battling the monster house, the main characters also battle their inner fears and conflicts. As the film progresses, DJ attempts to play many different roles as if he is trying on a range of different identities to see which one fits him best. From being cool and laid back, to acting caring and compassionate, he tries to impress Jenny with his fake bravado and problem-solving skills. In doing so, he moves from being a terrified child who constantly flees from Mr. Nebbercracker to a resilient adolescent who eventually protects and saves Mr. Nebbercracker from the very thing he loves most in this world, namely his departed wife whose hurt and anger is symbolized by the destructive nature of the monster house.

Monster House is a frighteningly good time, wrapping adolescent struggles in a gothic story that blends solid character development with fantastic special effects. In undertaking this perilous journey to battle a supernatural power—in venturing inside the monster house and discovering hidden secrets about Mr. Nebbercracker's past—the three characters break free from the safety and stability of their own homes and become more aware of how the greater world functions.

Why You Should See This Film: Because it's a delightful mixture of horror and comedy, filled with strong imagery and important lessons on friendship.

Main Themes: Teamwork * Heroism * Empathy * Courage * Fear

Classic Line: "Calm down! You make me want to throw up in some tin foil and eat it!"

Recommended Double Feature: *The Monster Squad* (1987); Rated PG-13, 82 minutes, Horror-adventure

MY BODYGUARD
(1980)

Directed by: Tony Bill
Written by: Alan Ormsby
Cast: Chris Makepeace (Clifford), Adam Baldwin (Ricky), Matt Dillon (Moody), Hank Salas (Mike)
Rating: Rated PG for violence and language
Runtime: 97 minutes
Genre: Drama

The Gist: What makes this film so special is not just its realistic depiction of bullying, but its portrayal of believable characters who struggle to fit in. Clifford Peache is a fifteen-year-old sophomore in high school who lives with his father and grandmother in downtown Chicago. The three of them live in the Ambassador hotel because Clifford's father is the manager. His grandmother is a bit eccentric and flirts with older men at the bar. His father—busy dealing with the guests and his own staff—is not a regular presence. Still, their brief interactions reveal a strong family unit based on trust and honesty. Clifford himself is your average teenager. He's not especially strong or good looking, but he is friendly and well mannered.

Clifford begins his first day of school as a new student at Lake View High School. Unlike the rest of the students, he arrives in a limousine. It's clear that most of the students are lower to middle class, and Clifford immediately stands out as being different. He soon learns that a bully named

Moody runs the school. He steals students' lunch money and also makes them pay him protection money so he won't beat them up. To make himself appear more righteous, Moody claims he is protecting everyone from another student named Ricky Linderman.

Clifford stands up for himself on the first day of school, angering Moody and his gang. They bully him in the bathroom later that afternoon, but he escapes. These early scenes at Lake View High School are effective in showing how bullies gain their power by gathering in numbers, and how they maintain their control because people are afraid to fight back. Clifford, however, does not let Moody and his gang intimidate him. In fact, he refuses to give them his money. This decision endears him to viewers because he acts with poise and confidence. In that moment, Clifford defends not only himself, but everyone who suffers from being bullied.

But then, being a concerned parent, Clifford's father calls the principal to report the harassment. Moody swears revenge on Clifford and

Chris Makepeace, Adam Baldwin. *20th Century-Fox/Photofest © 20th Century Fox*

begins to bother him on a daily basis. He and his friends dump food on his school clothes while he's in gym class. They trip him in the cafeteria. They shove him inside a locker. It's here that the film becomes much more than just a battle between Clifford and Moody. Instead, it develops a special friendship between Clifford and Ricky Linderman, an outcast student whom everyone fears even more than Moody.

There are rampant rumors surrounding Ricky Linderman. Some students say he's a psychopath and that he murdered several people. That he hangs out in a slaughterhouse. That he raped a teacher and shot a cop. It's telling that even Moody is afraid of Linderman. What's interesting is that no one ever talks to Linderman. People judge him unfairly because he is a hulking student who never smiles. Unlike Moody, he spends most of his time sitting by himself, immersed in his own thoughts. He is misunderstood because no one has taken the time to get to know him on a personal level.

Clifford, however, doesn't want to be afraid of Linderman and he doesn't believe all of the stories. Eventually, he learns that Linderman is dealing with the death of his younger brother who died while playing at home with a loaded gun. Together, despite their differences, the two of them become friends. While Clifford lives in a posh hotel, Linderman lives in a poor section of Chicago. Their friendship shows the importance of talking openly rather than of gossiping. Neither one is afraid of labels. They are both lonely people who feel ostracized in different ways. Together, Clifford and Linderman comb scrapyards to find the right cylinder for a motorcycle that Linderman has been building for over a year. The completed motorcycle becomes a symbol of their strong friendship as they cruise the city streets and venture beyond into the countryside. There is a great sense of freedom in these motorcycle scenes, as if both characters are escaping from the conflicts in their lives.

Linderman becomes Clifford's bodyguard, but then Moody gets his own bodyguard named Mike. The events that unfold are not simply lessons in standing up for oneself, but reminders of how we tend to judge others based on appearances. Linderman is not a violent person by nature and would prefer to be left alone. And Clifford, while a sensitive person, is angry at Moody and enjoys the security in knowing that Linderman will protect him. Clifford's feelings are natural, though, because he has been humiliated at school and wants justice.

The film reminds us how powerful we feel when we harass other people, but how powerless we feel when other people intimidate us. Yet, it's also about understanding and being misunderstood. It's about establishing supportive connections. And it's about the reasons that teenagers resort to violence, as well as the various ways they respond to it, both positively and negatively.

Why You Should See This Film: Because it's a feel-good story that highlights the importance of standing up not only for yourself, but also for your friends.

Main Themes: Bullying * Grief * Empowerment * Friendship * Communication

Classic Line: "Feel under the desk. You got gum there dating back to Neanderthal times. The gum's not the worst. It's the boogers that freak me out. You get hepatitis from the fresh ones."

Recommended Double Feature: *School Ties* (1992); Rated PG-13, 107 minutes, Drama

NAPOLEON DYNAMITE
(2004)

Directed by: Jared Hess
Written by: Jared Hess and Jerusha Hess
Cast: Jon Heder (Napoleon), Jon Gries (Uncle Rico), Aaron Ruell (Kip), Efren Ramirez (Pedro), Tina Majorino (Deb), Sandy Martin (Grandma), Shondrella Avery (Lafawnduh)
Rating: Rated PG for thematic elements and language
Runtime: 96 minutes
Genre: Comedy

The Gist: The story centers on Napoleon Dynamite, a socially awkward teenager who lives in Preston, Idaho, with his grandmother and his older brother, Kip. His grandmother dotes on a llama named Tina and enjoys four-wheeling at the sand dunes. Kip is thirty-two years old and unemployed. He spends his days in internet chat rooms, hoping to find his soul mate. He's also training to be a cage fighter, which is hilarious because he's thin and scrawny and enjoys eating nachos. The characters are nerdy and inexperienced, but they're endearing because of their naïveté and goofiness. They talk slowly, as if they're perpetually bored. Both weird and charming in equal doses, the film is a parody of small-town America.

Napoleon is immature, but amusing. He carries a card in his wallet titled "UFO Abduction Insurance," claims to know secret ninja moves, and likes to stash tater tots in the side pocket of his cargo pants. He also likes to draw pictures of people and imaginary animals, like a liger, which

Efren Ramirez, Jon Heder. ***Fox Searchlight Pictures/Photofest © Fox Searchlight Pictures***

he tells people is a cross between a lion and tiger. Napoleon doesn't have many friends at school. Instead, he is shoved into lockers and taunted by the other students. His only friends are Pedro—a new student who has just transferred from Juarez, Mexico—and Deb, a shy girl who goes door to door promoting her glamour shot business and selling trinkets like key chains so she can pay for college.

During the opening scenes, Napoleon gets on the school bus and sits at the very back. He then digs into his backpack and pulls out an action figure tied to a piece of string. He tosses the action figure out the window and holds the string in his hand, watching as the action figure bounces on the road behind the school bus. This mindless activity illustrates Napoleon's idea of entertainment. He fantasizes constantly and tells outrageous lies to look cool, like claiming he spent the summer hunting wolverines in Alaska. It's clear he lives out adventures in his mind because his daily life is unexciting.

When his grandmother breaks her coccyx during one of her four-wheeling adventures, Uncle Rico arrives to stay at the house while she recovers. Uncle Rico lives in an orange campervan. He misses the glory days of his high school years and says that back in 1982 he could throw a football a quarter mile. Uncle Rico records himself throwing terrible football passes and acting like a star quarterback. He desperately wants to travel back in time, and he actually buys a time machine online, which supplies one of the film's funniest scenes. Napoleon hates that Uncle Rico is always hanging around the house. His uncle's presence reminds Napoleon that nobody thinks he and Kip can take care of themselves.

Each of the main characters is lonely in his or her own way, but as the story unfolds they all become involved in various types of relationships. Napoleon spends time with Deb, though his flirting is often awkward. He also supports her businesses and shares a tender moment with her at the school dance. Deb has a habit of not looking people in the eye when she speaks, but it's clear that when she hangs around Napoleon she smiles more and her voice is louder. She feels comfortable in his presence because she knows he won't judge her like everyone else.

Napoleon also becomes closer with Pedro, helping him to run for class president. At first, Pedro is hesitant because he is running against one of the most popular girls in the school. When Pedro asks Napoleon if he thinks anyone will vote for him, Napoleon tries to boost his friend's confidence by saying, "You have a sweet bike. And you're really good at hooking up with chicks. Plus, you're like the only guy at school who has a mustache." Napoleon's loyalty to Pedro culminates in him performing a wildly entertaining dance number in front of the entire school. While his antics are often ridiculous, no one can deny that Napoleon is fearless.

Kip is lazy and soft spoken at the beginning of the film. He asks Napoleon to pull him into town, which involves Kip strapping on in-line skates and holding on to a rope as Napoleon rides his bike. Kip is very much a homebody, and it's his online relationship with a woman from Detroit named Lafawnduh that changes his life. She eventually visits Kip and proves to be an important influence. She helps Kip to find love and to become more confident in himself. Their relationship celebrates the power of taking chances and of stepping out of one's comfort zone.

Napoleon Dynamite is a deadpan comedy that finds its humor more in the characters than in the situations. This is not a film in which the characters follow the plot. Rather, it's one in which the characters themselves create awkward and realistic moments that typify the confusion and anxiety of the high school years.

Why You Should See This Film: Because it's an epic celebration of geekhood, stuffed with quirky dialogue and eccentric characters.

Main Themes: Family * Self-Confidence * Apathy * Responsibility * Acceptance

Classic Line: "Nunchuck skills, bowhunting skills, computer hacking skills. Girls only want boyfriends who have great skills."

Recommended Double Feature: *Ghost World* (2001); Rated R, 112 minutes, Drama-comedy

ORANGE COUNTY
(2002)

Directed by: Jake Kasdan
Written by: Mike White
Cast: Colin Hanks (Shaun), Jack Black (Lance), Schuyler Fisk (Ashley), John Lithgow (Bud), Catherine O'Hara (Cindy)
Rating: Rated PG-13 for drug content, language, and sexuality
Runtime: 87 minutes
Genre: Comedy

The Gist: Shaun Brumder lives in Orange County, California. He's an intelligent student who succeeds in high school without putting forth much effort. He spends his carefree days surfing, playing volleyball, drinking beer, partying around bonfires, and hanging out with his girlfriend, Ashley. His family is hilarious yet dysfunctional: a stoner brother (Lance), an alcoholic mother (Cindy), and a father (Bud) who is married to a much younger woman. Shaun doesn't consider the future too much. He idly moves from one day to the next. But when his friend dies in a surfing accident, he reflects on his own life and begins to wonder if there is a higher purpose.

Around this traumatic time, Shaun discovers the novel *Strait Jacket* by Marcus Skinner, which is buried in the sand at the beach. He reads the book once, then reads it over and over again, amazed at how it completely captures what it means to be a teenager. After reading the book fifty times in one month, Shaun finally decides he wants to become a writer. He vows to attend Stanford University so he can study creative writing with Marcus Skinner. Immediately, he turns his life around by earning a 4.0 during his senior year, boasting a 1520 on the SAT, and becoming the class president.

One of the reasons Shaun wants to leave Orange County is because there is no one around to give him constructive criticism and feedback. He needs a more nurturing environment. He feels like the people around him are holding him back. Shaun is convinced that to achieve greatness he needs to separate himself from everything that is familiar and stable. Ashley is smart and sensitive, but she is also overly complimentary. Lance seems high and disinterested most of the time. And Shaun's mother refuses to acknowledge that he will leave home to go to college. At one point, his English teacher hands back a written assignment and admits that he didn't read it because it was too long. Shaun is looking for inspiration to feed his creative energy, but he views most of his classmates as superficial. They're more interested in themselves than in the power of the arts.

Of course, everything up until this point in the story is related during the first few minutes of the film, during which Shaun types his college application letter to Marcus Skinner. In a voice-over, he relates the story of how he discovered *Strait Jacket* and how he began writing every day. He presents his hometown as a unique place full of quirky characters. He then proclaims the esteemed author a genius and ends the letter by telling him how much he looks forward to meeting him in the fall. This introduction is emotional because Shaun is seeing a clear path to his future for the first time in his life. No longer content to lounge around, he has found a purpose. His excitement mirrors adolescents who begin the process of applying to colleges and processing the idea of life after high school.

But his dreams of attending Stanford are derailed when his guidance counselor submits the wrong application and he receives a rejection letter in the mail. The rest of the film follows Shaun's attempts to gain entrance into the prestigious university. These involve a series of hilarious complications. His wacky family unintentionally sabotages his meeting with a member of the alumni board; Lance drives him to Stanford so he can plead his case to the dean of admissions; and he attends a college party in which he discovers that the students are not that much different from his classmates back in Orange County.

The film deals with the desire that many teenagers face in wanting to leave home to find themselves. In many ways, Shaun's overwhelming urge to leave his hometown is also an urge to escape his family. He's become tired of predictability, and he wants to experience new people and adventures. Added to this, no one seems to take him seriously. His father, upon hearing Shaun's desire to be a novelist, says, "A writer? What do you have to write about? You're not oppressed. You're not gay." His friends don't want to talk about books because they prefer to spend all of their time surfing. And his English teacher refuses to call on him, even when Shaun's hand is the only one raised.

While the film is funny and tender, it also illustrates the importance of the arts and humanities. Shaun's life seems to be stuck in a rut until he finds *Strait Jacket*, whereupon he relates to the novel's main character and realizes there's a larger world beyond Orange County. It's through writing that he is able to make connections with other works of literature, and to build on relationships with his friends and family. Though the majority of the film only takes place over a two-day period, Shaun experiences a lot of growth. He begins to understand that all of us, to some degree, struggle with where we have been and with where we are going.

Why You Should See This Film: Because it's a smart and funny portrayal of a laid-back bookworm who believes that going to college will solve all of life's problems.

Main Themes: Acceptance * Disillusionment * Family * Teamwork * Self-Awareness

Classic Line: "Look, Shaun, I'm sorry you didn't get into Stanford. But if you think that going here is the only way that you can be the person you want to be, then I just feel sorry for you."

Recommended Double Feature: *Adventures in Babysitting* (1987); Rated PG-13, 102 minutes, Comedy-adventure

THE PERKS OF BEING A WALLFLOWER
(2012)

Directed by: Stephen Chbosky
Written by: Stephen Chbosky, based on his novel
Cast: Logan Lerman (Charlie), Ezra Miller (Patrick), Emma Watson (Sam), Mae Whitman (Mary Elizabeth), Paul Rudd (Mr. Anderson)
Rating: Rated PG-13 for mature thematic material, drug and alcohol use, sexual content, and mild violence
Runtime: 105 minutes
Genre: Drama

The Gist: This is a touching film about the power of friendship. It focuses on a lonely student named Charlie who begins his freshman year of high school with no friends. He struggles with a past trauma in his life and seems anxious most of the time. He is clinically depressed and prone to blackouts. Yet amid all the sorrow and despair—despite the bullying and misunderstandings—the film also shows how decent and good-hearted people can make a difference in our lives if we're brave enough to give them the opportunity.

Throughout the film, Charlie writes a series of letters that he addresses to "Dear Friend." It's unclear who exactly this recipient is, but it doesn't matter. Whether he is writing to an actual person, or perhaps just composing the letters to satisfy his subconscious, Charlie writes them so he can talk seriously about his life. He wants to understand why certain things are happening to him, such as other students teasing him or his middle school friends no longer acknowledging him. In writing about the details of his own quiet life, Charlie explores how he can best respond to those awkward situations. If he takes control of them, or even eliminates them, then perhaps he can feel more normal and less like an outsider.

Charlie admits he needs to turn things around. He wants to move past the difficulties in his life, and he hopes to acquire a new identity by shedding his old one. Nevertheless, he is alienated from his peers and made fun of throughout his first day of high school. He is so shy that he doesn't answer the teacher's questions in his English class, even though he knows all of the answers. At lunch, Charlie sits by himself in the cafeteria, observing everyone around him.

But then he meets two seniors—Patrick and his stepsister Sam—at a football game. They invite him to a party. For the first time since beginning high school, he feels included. Patrick and Sam show a genuine interest in Charlie. They want to learn more about him. They ask him questions and treat him kindly. At the party, Sam is saddened when Charlie tells her that his friend killed himself the year before. Realizing he has no friends, Patrick makes a short speech and then everyone at the party toasts Charlie.

Emma Watson, Logan Lerman. ***Summit Entertainment/Photofest © Summit Entertainment***

Patrick calls him a wallflower, someone who sits off to the side by himself and doesn't talk much. Charlie is moved by the attention and says he didn't think anyone noticed him. This scene is special in several ways. Charlie now becomes friends with a close-knit group of people who are as eclectic as he is. They appreciate him and enjoy hanging out with him. They eat lunch together at school and share their musical tastes. They attend numerous performances of *The Rocky Horror Picture Show*. As well, the love that this group shows toward Charlie reflects the type of friendship everyone hopes to find during adolescence.

What's refreshing about this small group of friends is that they don't act like a typical clique. They aren't selfish and striving for popularity. They don't make fun of other people or even worry what other people say about them. They care about and are interested in each other instead of caring about how much their classmates are interested in them. They are also smart characters who are conscious of their past mistakes. More importantly, they learn from those mistakes and try to improve their lives. For example, Sam admits she partied too hard during her freshman year and wishes she could have earned better grades.

Charlie becomes happier and more expressive. At one point, referencing advice his doctor gave him, Charlie says, "We can't choose where we come from, but we can choose where we go from there." His new friendships have instilled in him a confidence that makes him realize he can control the choices in his life. And when he falls in love with Sam, his newfound confidence pushes him to impress her even though she has a boyfriend. But Charlie must also contend with Mary Elizabeth, another member of their group who has a crush on him.

Confused, he tries hard to love Mary Elizabeth because he heard that having a girlfriend makes one happy. In addition to developing new friendships and a social life, he is now figuring out how to be in an intimate relationship. As the pressures mount, he begins to relapse. He becomes depressed again. Part of his anxiety stems from knowing that at the end of the school year they will all leave for college. He depends on these people, and without them he will be forced to seek out new friends. Eventually, Charlie must confront his past trauma and process it in a healthy way. As with everyone, he needs to understand that just because something happens to us, that doesn't mean we have to let it define us.

Why You Should See This Film: Because it's an inspiring story that addresses serious issues while offering a poignant look at the power of inclusion.

Main Themes: Acceptance * Friendship * Grief * Self-Confidence * Courage

Classic Line: "We accept the love we think we deserve."

Recommended Double Feature: *Short Term 12* (2013); Rated R, 97 minutes, Drama

PRETTY IN PINK
(1986)

Directed by: Howard Deutch
Written by: John Hughes
Cast: Molly Ringwald (Andie), Harry Dean Stanton (Jack), Jon Cryer (Duckie), James Spader (Steff), Andrew McCarthy (Blane)
Rating: Rated PG-13 for adult situations and language
Runtime: 96 minutes
Genre: Romantic comedy

The Gist: This is one of the seminal films from the 1980s. It's the classic story of a poor girl and a rich boy who fall in love and struggle to be together. But despite these obvious clichés, the film is a love letter to the music and fashions that defined an entire generation. The screenplay is insightful in the way it sets up a love triangle involving the three main characters: Andie, Blane, and Duckie. It presents internal and external struggles that reveal high school as a crucial time in understanding the value of friendship, as well as the dangers inherent in judging other people based on their appearance.

Andie lives in a lower-class neighborhood with her unemployed father, Jack. Her mother left years ago, and it's apparent from the beginning that she manages the household all by herself. She wakes up her father every morning and brings him coffee. She instructs him to shower and encourages him to find a job. Their relationship, however, is not awkward or hostile. Instead, he appreciates everything his daughter does for them.

He also takes the time to sit down and talk with Andie. He asks her about school, and if she's been invited to the prom. Whereas other films might use class structure to create tension between adolescents and their parents, *Pretty in Pink* reveals that it's only a cause for concern because the adolescents make it one.

Andie dreams of a better life. She makes her own clothes to save money, and she drives through the rich neighborhoods to admire the houses. It's clear that her need to act as a provider at home has made her more aware of her social status. This is especially true at school where she is attracted to a good-looking and popular student named Blane. Unlike Andie, Blane is upper class. He wears fancy clothes and drives a BMW. But he's also a nice guy. They are attracted to each other, but Andie is unsure whether she should date him. She doesn't know if he will accept her because her family doesn't have money. Her father, always supportive, tells her the most important thing is that they both like each other.

Conflicted, Andie asks some of her friends if they would ever consider going out with someone who has money. At the same time, Blane's friend Steff constantly dumps on Andie because she's poor. Steff is spoiled and conceited. He brags about all the girls he's dated. He despises Andie's poverty, but he is also angry because she refuses to go out with him. Steff believes he is entitled to anything and anyone because of his upper-class status. He is especially angry because he can't understand why someone who has no money would refuse to be with someone who is rich. When Steff realizes that Blane likes Andie, he tells his friend he is wasting his time on her. Steff proclaims that Andie will always amount to nothing.

These serious discussions—whether between Blane and his friends or between Andie and her friends—illustrate that appearance and perception are important to most adolescents. They care deeply about their friends' opinions, sometimes to such an extreme that they sabotage their own happiness. In deciding who they should spend time with, they often consider not just their own feelings, but how their friends will react. For example, when Andie and Blane finally agree to go out on a date, she is so ashamed of where she lives that she asks him to pick her up at the record store where she works.

Mixed into all of this drama is Duckie. He and Andie are close friends who have known each other for years. Duckie has a crush on her. He constantly jokes with her as if they were in a relationship. Though he is funny and outgoing, he still struggles with how to tell Andie that he loves her. In one of the film's more heartfelt scenes, he tells her father that he plans to marry her. Jack smiles and explains to Duckie that he can love Andie, but that doesn't mean she will love him back. Jack's response is not angry, but honest and realistic. He seems to empathize with Duckie because he and Andie are still struggling with his wife's absence.

Sometimes, however, Duckie can be just as much of a jerk as Blane's friends. In this way, he is similar to Steff, although they both express their anger differently. Duckie is hurt that Andie likes Blane, and he distances himself from her because he can't stand to see her with someone who is rich and popular. He is afraid Blane will hurt Andie, but he also feels rejected because they've spent so much time together. Andie, who is frustrated by everyone around her, tells her father, "I just want them to know that they didn't break me." Her character serves as a positive example for adolescents who refuse to let labels and biases affect how they treat others.

The film combines humor and drama effectively to show the intolerance that exists among various cliques and classes. Blane and Andie must decide if they want to pursue love and risk losing their friends, or if they want to ignore their escalating attraction and hold on to their friends. In doing so, they also need to consider if those friendships are worth keeping.

Why You Should See This Film: Because it's a sweet and sentimental story about two teenagers trying to overcome social standards and insecurities.

Main Themes: Jealousy * Communication * Prejudice * Selfishness * Class

Classic Line: "It's called a sense of humor. You should get one. They're nice."

Recommended Double Feature: *Some Kind of Wonderful* (1987); Rated PG-13, 95 minutes, Drama-romance

PRINCESS CYD
(2017)

Directed by: Stephen Cone
Written by: Stephen Cone
Cast: Jessie Pinnick (Cyd), Rebecca Spence (Miranda), Malic White (Katie), James Vincent Meredith (Anthony)
Rating: Not rated by the MPAA, though it does contain brief nudity, language, sexuality, and some drug use
Runtime: 96 minutes
Genre: Drama-romance

The Gist: This is a small independent film with a big heart. It's an uplifting character study about two women who grow to respect and understand each other over the course of a few weeks. One of those women is Cyd, a sixteen-year-old who plays soccer and lives in South Carolina with her father. The other woman is her estranged aunt Miranda, a famous author who lives in Chicago. Cyd's mother died nine years earlier, and her father is always depressed. Because they argue a lot, they both agree that Cyd should visit Miranda so she can explore colleges.

The film is cheerful and inspiring despite its somber opening moments. A 911 call plays over a black screen as a neighbor informs the police there has been an accident next door. He tells the officer he has discovered some bodies, and the only person he mentions as having survived is a little girl. Aside from this tragic moment, the death of Cyd's mother is not discussed in great detail. There are a few mentions of her throughout the film—a room she slept in or a book she once read—but they are not steeped in grand, dramatic moments. Instead, their placement reminds us of the family's loss while highlighting the importance of Cyd and Miranda's relationship.

The two women have isolated themselves within their own lives. At the beginning of the film, it's clear they don't know how to relate to each other. In fact, Miranda worries that Cyd will find her boring. While Miranda loves to read and discuss literature, Cyd doesn't enjoy books. At one point, she asks Miranda to explain her new novel, and when Miranda hesitates because she doesn't want to spoil it, Cyd tells her it's okay because she doesn't plan to read it. While these initial talks are brief and awkward, they eventually create a comfort level between the two women that leads to richer conversations on topics like sex and religion.

Both women have struggles in their personal relationships. Cyd has a boyfriend back in South Carolina, but she speaks of him as more of a hobby than as a passion. While in Chicago, she meets Katie, who is working in a coffee shop. There is an immediate and mutual attraction, despite the fact that Cyd is unsure how to act around Katie. These scenes are realistic in showing the confusion and uncertainty in forging new relationships. Eventually, their flirtations blossom into a touching romance.

Cyd's feelings toward Katie strengthen her bond with Miranda. When Cyd confides in her aunt that she finds Katie attractive and wants to have sex with her, Miranda doesn't judge her or lecture her. She listens and validates her niece's emotions. Their conversations also result in Miranda admitting she hasn't had an intimate relationship in several years because she's devoted herself to her writing. She does spend time with her friend Anthony, a nonfiction journalist who visits her regularly to workshop his first novel. But Miranda doesn't begin to view Anthony as a potential love interest until she and Cyd begin talking about love and sex.

What's more, it's not until the two women begin to have heartfelt conversations that their personal attitudes change. After Cyd lies outside to tan, Miranda digs out her old bathing suit and joins her in the backyard, acting young and hip. And following their talk on love, Miranda stands naked in front of a full-length mirror, studying herself to gauge her attractiveness. Likewise, Cyd begins to view her aunt as cool. She's surprised when strangers approach Miranda and ask her for an autograph. She also learns that her aunt wrote a book called *Princess Cydney*, which reveals more about her family's past. These revelations reveal how little Cyd knows about her family because she has never taken the time to ask any important questions.

At the beginning of the film, Cyd asks Miranda, "Do you ever wish you moved away? Like, tried other cities?" She thinks it's strange that her aunt is living in the same city she grew up in. Cyd's pointed question illustrates the desire many adolescents have to leave home so they can separate from their parents and be more independent. But Cyd is naïve and believes familiarity is stifling. She doesn't understand the crucial role a physical location can play in helping to form one's values and personality.

Leaving home provides Cyd with the opportunities she needs to express herself and to explore who she is and who she wants to be. Those looking for a fast-paced film might be disappointed, but those who appreciate an introspective character study will find *Princess Cyd* engrossing. It's a quiet and moving story about female sexuality and two generations of women who influence each other in surprising ways.

Why You Should See This Film: Because this is a film about listening and understanding, as well as about the healing power of family and friendship.

Main Themes: Acceptance * Sexual Discovery * Grief * Communication * Love

Classic Line: "It is not a handicap to have one thing but not another. To be one way and not another. We are different shapes and ways, and our happiness is unique. There are no rules of balance."

Recommended Double Feature: *The Way He Looks* (2014); Not Rated, 96 minutes, Drama-romance

RAISING VICTOR VARGAS
(2002)

Directed by: Peter Sollett
Written by: Peter Sollett
Cast: Victor Rasuk (Victor), Judy Marte (Judy), Altagracia Guzman (Grandma), Silvestre Rasuk (Nino), Krystal Rodriguez (Vicki), Melonie Diaz (Melonie), Kevin Rivera (Harold)
Rating: Rated R for strong language
Runtime: 88 minutes
Genre: Drama-romance

The Gist: This is a touching story about family bonds and adolescent romance. It centers on a Latino family who lives in a poor neighborhood in the Lower East Side of New York City. The head of the family is Grandma, a strict and deeply religious woman who is raising her three grandchildren: Victor, Nino, and Vicki. Victor is the main character, a brash sixteen-year-old who is inexperienced in the ways of love but still believes he is an irresistible heartthrob. Nino is an accomplished piano player who idolizes Victor and is always asking his older brother for advice about girls. Vicki, who enjoys gossiping, spends most of her time sitting on the couch and watching TV.

Victor flirts constantly with women. He tells them they have never been with a man until they've been with him. He is overconfident because he is immature and unsure of himself. Victor is a private person who doesn't want anyone else to know his business. He is afraid of other people judging his actions, and he cares more about his image than about developing a real relationship. This is evident at the beginning of the film when people make fun of him for hooking up with a woman who lives in his apartment building and is considered unattractive.

Then Victor sees Judy at the community pool and decides to pursue her. She is beautiful and sought after by all of the men in their neighborhood. In fact, she is known as Juicy Judy. But Judy isn't interested in a relationship and she continuously ignores Victor's advances. She lies and tells him she has boyfriend, thinking he will go away. Judy thinks all men are dogs because of the sexual and derogatory remarks they make toward her on a daily basis. Victor is determined to win Judy, however, and eventually she agrees to hang out with him. She hopes the other men will leave her alone if they see her hanging around with Victor. Judy refers to him as bug spray, which shows her disinterest in getting to know him on a more personal level.

Victor and Judy are similar in that both characters value their personal space and wish to lead private lives. It's clear they are afraid of sacrificing their individuality by becoming involved in a serious relationship. Because of this fear, they are extremely careful in sharing their feelings. At one point, Victor tells Judy, "What we do is between me and you." Both of them are good people, but their lack of intimate experiences has made them awkward in romantic situations. While Judy is more interested in using Victor as a shield against other men, he seems more interested in bragging about the fact that he is now dating the elusive and much-sought-after Judy.

Further complicating Victor's life is Grandma. She has a good heart, but her grandchildren are growing up and becoming interested in dating. As a result, there is a generational divide that creates conflicts in their apartment. Grandma thinks Victor is a bad influence on the other two children. She doesn't want him introducing men to his sister, and she's concerned when Nino begins spending extra time in the bathroom because he's going through puberty. She also makes it a point to tell the three children that she is the only thing they have. She continuously asks them to be a good family, and she takes them all to church so they can light candles and pray.

Despite what Grandma says, it's obvious she needs her three grandchildren just as much as they need her. They might be impulsive and im-

Victor Rasuk, Judy Marte. ***Samuel Goldwyn Company/Photofest © Samuel Goldwyn Company***

mature, perhaps a bit selfish, but they are also confused teenagers. Though the three of them often fight and argue—misbehaving so as to test the boundaries of their independence—they love their grandma. Whenever she becomes upset, they feel guilty and assure her they will try to be more considerate and obedient. As Victor's relationship with Judy develops, he begins to understand more his responsibilities at home. He realizes that as the oldest child he must help Grandma. He must be a provider instead of a burden.

Intercut with Victor and Judy's relationship is a sweet romance between Victor's friend Harold and Judy's friend Melonie. Unlike Victor and Judy, Harold and Melonie talk honestly with each other. They are not afraid to say what they are feeling. Their awkwardness is touching whereas Victor and Judy's awkwardness is troubling. The importance of Harold and Melonie's relationship is that it offers a glimpse of the intimacy Victor and Judy could enjoy if they both learned to trust each other and not be so guarded.

Raising Victor Vargas is funny and dramatic in its portrayal of family conflicts and first love. It presents characters who speak and act like real teenagers. They have normal frustrations and desires, but they are intelligent and observant. Their struggles to fit in and grow up are not just with other people, but also with themselves.

Why You Should See This Film: Because it's a realistic inner-city romance, full of thoughtful and tender moments, that avoids the usual clichés of gangs and violence.

Main Themes: Honesty * Family * Responsibility * Insecurity * Self-Awareness

Classic Line: "Okay, you're my new man. But I'm warning you. Don't fuck with me."

Recommended Double Feature: *Boyz n the Hood* (1991); Rated R, 112 minutes, Drama

READY PLAYER ONE
(2018)

Directed by: Steven Spielberg
Written by: Zak Penn and Ernest Cline, based on the novel by Ernest Cline
Cast: Tye Sheridan (Parzival/Wade), Olivia Cooke (Art3mis/Samantha), Brian Mendelsohn (Sorrento), Mark Rylance (Halliday)
Rating: Rated PG-13 for sequences of sci-fi action violence, bloody images, some suggestive material, partial nudity, and language
Runtime: 140 minutes
Genre: Science fiction–adventure

The Gist: This is an action-packed adventure loaded with great-looking CGI and hundreds of references from the 1980s and 1990s. Part of the fun in watching the film comes from spotting classic merchandise and fashions—like the Atari 2600—as well as recognizing references to classic film directors like James Cameron, John Hughes, and Robert Zemeckis. It's not every day you see a film that contains a He-Man lunchbox, King Kong, the DeLorean from *Back to the Future*, the Iron Giant, and the murderous Chucky from the *Child's Play* movies.

The year is 2045 in Columbus, Ohio. Teenager Wade Watts lives in the Stacks with his aunt and her loser boyfriend. The Stacks is an ugly collection of shacks piled atop one another like a massive dump. Everything looks gray and washed out. There is sense of hopelessness associated with the lower-class people living in the Stacks. However, the film also opens to the tune of Van Halen's song "Jump," which is lively and upbeat. The joyfulness of the rock-and-roll music contradicts the desolate imagery seen on-screen.

The vast majority of songs are from the 1980s: "You Make My Dreams," "Everybody Wants to Rule the World," and "We're Not Gonna Take It," to name a few. These songs energize the film, much of which takes place in a virtual reality world called the OASIS. The OASIS is a diversion from life in the Stacks. Despite the close proximity forced upon people by overcrowded slums, they don't converse with one another. Instead, they wear assorted video game apparel (suits, eyeglasses, and controllers) because they spend most of their time inside of the OASIS while disguised as a virtual avatar.

As the film begins, Wade narrates the story of how the OASIS was created by James Donovan Halliday. Before his death, he announced Anorak's game, which involves unraveling a series of clues to find three secret keys and ultimately win a golden Easter egg. The winner is awarded half a trillion dollars and total control of the OASIS. The first key can only be claimed by winning a street race through a virtual city. This involves dodging various obstacles, as well as avoiding the wrath of King Kong and a Tyrannosaurus Rex. When Wade— disguised as his avatar named Parzival—figures out the secret to winning the race, he becomes an instant celebrity and begins a quest to find the three keys and to win the game.

Wade enlists the help of several friends, including a plucky girl known as Art3mis whose real name is Samantha. They must work together to solve the clues. They are being pursued by Nolan Sorrento, the CEO of Innovative Online Industries (IOI). Sorrento is power hungry and wants to win the game himself so he can control the OASIS. The film is also a love story between Wade (Parzival) and Samantha (Art3mis). While their budding romance is secondary to the action, it's important to recognize how playing the game creates mutual trust that helps them to survive against Sorrento and his cronies. In a competition, people can sometimes be selfish and unhelpful, but Anorak's game has larger implications relating to class, the economy, and personal independence. There is more at stake than a cash prize and unlimited bragging rights.

The OASIS is emblematic of our imaginations, a realm where anything is possible. Inside the OASIS, people can construct a new identity and live a completely different life. People who are weak can be strong.

People who are shy can be assertive. And people who are unhappy with their physical features can choose to disguise themselves as an attractive avatar. These possibilities make *Ready Player One* especially appealing to teenagers who are still in the process of constructing their self-identities. Sometimes, playing a video game, watching a film, or listening to a song can empower us and create opportunities that enrich our lives.

Ready Player One is an exhilarating scavenger hunt that draws us into the story until we feel like we're playing Anorak's game right alongside the main characters. Like a video game, there are multiple levels to the film. There are also multiple levels to each character: his or her true identity and the avatar that he or she assumes while inside the OASIS. There are also two alternating planes on which the characters find themselves, namely the real world and the virtual world. It's fascinating to discover how all of these levels continuously impact each other as the narrative unfolds, and as the stakes become more and more dangerous.

The art design of the OASIS is beautiful, creating a world of magic and wonder. Yes, it's more pleasing and exciting than the real world, but one of the film's messages is that virtual reality cannot be a constant escape. As Wade remains steadfast in his determination to solve each clue, and to deal with increasing obstacles, he becomes a symbol of freedom and individuality, not just to those who want to see him win or lose the game, but to anyone who has ever worked hard and striven to succeed.

Why You Should See This Film: Because it's a dazzling and nostalgic mashup of pop culture and video games, brimming with fervent energy.

Main Themes: Survival * War * Teamwork * Oppression * Perseverance

Classic Line: "It's not about winning. It's about playing."

Recommended Double Feature: *WarGames* (1983); Rated PG, 114 minutes, Science fiction–thriller

REBEL WITHOUT A CAUSE
(1955)

Directed by: Nicholas Ray
Written by: Stewart Stern
Cast: James Dean (Jim), Natalie Wood (Judy), Sal Mineo (Plato), Jim Backus (Frank), William Hopper (Judy's father)
Rating: Rated PG-13 for moderate violence, alcohol use, and smoking
Runtime: 111 minutes
Genre: Drama

The Gist: The story focuses on three characters—Jim, Judy, and Plato—who struggle with being individuals while fighting against their parents' expectations. The film's title was adapted from a book by psychiatrist Robert M. Lindner titled *Rebel without a Cause: The Hypnoanalysis of a Criminal Psychopath*. Though the film may be considered tame to contemporary audiences, it does present a realistic window through which to view an adolescent lifestyle in 1950s America.

The opening shot shows a drunken Jim lying on the ground with a bemused expression. He plays with a toy and a crumpled-up newspaper. His hands grasp at whatever is in his vicinity. He seems lost, and in a touching move that foreshadows his decency and goodness, he uses the newspaper like a blanket to cover up the toy. Our first introduction to this emotionally troubled teenager is when he's vulnerable and lying flat on the ground, as if he's hit rock bottom.

The beginning scenes occur in a police station late at night. Each of the film's three main characters are introduced, and each character is shown to have significant family problems. Judy talks about how much her father hates her. She believes he has a low opinion of her and doesn't like her friends. She is upset because he called her a tramp. Jim is angry because his parents fight all the time. He thinks his father is weak because he doesn't stand up to his mother. Plato, whose real name is John Crawford, lives with the family's housekeeper. His father abandoned them all when Plato was younger. His mother is absent most of the time.

Each of these characters feels lonely and abandoned. They don't understand how to process their anger and frustration. Jim is arrested for drunkenness, Judy is picked up for breaking curfew, and Plato is guilty of shooting some puppies. At the police station, Jim asks the psychiatrist to lock him up because he's afraid he's going to hit somebody. He pleads for help because he doesn't want to be violent. What sets Jim apart from other juvenile delinquents is his truthfulness. He wants to be a better person even if he doesn't know how to communicate with his parents or how to fix his problems.

The separation between the teenagers and their parents is clear from the beginning. Plato feels rejected at his parents' disinterest in his life. Judy feels rejected because her father is uncomfortable whenever she kisses him; he's unsure how to handle the fact that she's developing into a woman. And Jim feels rejected because his parents don't respect each other. Throughout the film, Jim tries to have philosophical conversations with his father—asking him questions about honesty and what it means to be a good person—but his father has difficulty relating to him. His response to Jim's behavior is to remind him that he buys his son everything he wants.

Sal Mineo, James Dean, Corey Allen. *Warner Bros./Photofest © Warner Bros.*

It also doesn't help that Jim is the new kid in town and trying to find a new group of friends. He also doesn't like being called a chicken. His sensitivity to name calling is no doubt fueled by the fact that he perceives his own father as weak. When another student taunts him during a school trip to a planetarium, Jim becomes involved in a knife fight and later races in a game of chicken with some stolen cars. Because of their unhappy home lives, the characters spend as little time as possible with their families. They seek out other settings that afford them the safety and stability they crave. One of these places is the planetarium. During one scene, Jim looks up at the shimmering stars and says to Plato, "Once you've been up there, you know you've been someplace." The planetarium represents freedom because inside the darkness there are infinite possibilities for the paths their lives can take.

Eventually, Jim befriends Judy and their relationship blossoms into a romance. Together, they spend time with Plato. In this way, the three of them form a close family unit that only accentuates the lack of love and attention they receive at home. To be sure, the film is sensational in its presentation of the conflicts that arise among parents, police, and teenagers. But these destructive relationships create a somber mood that helps to illustrate the importance of using effective communication to resolve problems.

It should be noted that the teenagers are not completely innocent. They make bad decisions that land them in the police station, and they often let their anger control them. They tend to be fragile in their emotions and quick to respond. Sometimes, they even sabotage their own happiness. In their impulsivity, they forget to stop for a moment and consider the possible consequences of their actions.

Why You Should See This Film: Because it's a classic melodrama about confused teenagers and the conflicts that erupt between generations.

Main Themes: Bullying * Family * Honesty * Rebelliousness * Oppression

Classic Line: "If I had one day when I didn't have to be all confused and I didn't have to feel that I was ashamed of everything. If I felt that I belonged someplace. You know?"

Recommended Double Feature: *The 400 Blows* (1959); Not Rated, 99 minutes, Drama

RISKY BUSINESS
(1983)

Directed by: Paul Brickman
Written by: Paul Brickman
Cast: Tom Cruise (Joel), Rebecca De Mornay (Lana), Joe Pantoliano (Guido), Curtis Armstrong (Miles)
Rating: Rated R for adult situations, language, and nudity
Runtime: 99 minutes
Genre: Comedy-drama

The Gist: Here is an intelligent comedy that explores important themes like guilt and sex from an adolescent perspective. The story centers on Joel, a high school senior who lives in an upper-class suburb in Chicago. Like most students, he is worried about being accepted into a good university. His father wants him to attend Princeton University, his alma mater. Because of this pressure to succeed, Joel studies hard and is a member of several prominent clubs, including Future Enterprisers in which students work together in groups to create small businesses. In fact, the first conversation he has with his mother in the film concerns his SAT scores. But when Joel's parents leave town on a trip, he goes too far in celebrating his newfound independence, which leads to several wild incidents.

The film illustrates the many stresses involved in surviving high school, such as developing intimate relationships, acing college exams, and dealing with parental rules. It also shows the anxiety caused by expecting teenagers to start planning for their futures before they've even considered what exactly they hope to accomplish. The opening scene establishes Joel's constant worry and paranoia. He has a dream in which he enters his neighbor's house and discovers a beautiful woman in the shower. Upon walking into the steamy stall, he suddenly finds himself in a crowded classroom where he is three hours late for a college-entrance exam.

This dream sequence reveals Joel's fear that he will never be accepted into a prestigious university. Joel doesn't have a girlfriend, and it's clear that he views sex as an obstacle in achieving his goals. He says, "I don't want to make a mistake and jeopardize my future." He is afraid that engaging in any sexual activity will potentially ruin his life by affecting his grade point average. Clearly, Joel believes he should be spending all of his time on studying for final exams and preparing for his interview with a Princeton admissions officer. His sexual fantasies create intense feelings of shame and guilt. For example, another dream sequence, in which he romances a babysitter, ends with the police surrounding the house.

Joel's lack of excitement in his life is noticed by his friend, Miles. He convinces Joel to take advantage of his parents leaving by adopting a "who cares" attitude. As a result, Joel drives his father's prized Porsche, raids the liquor cabinet, and blasts "Old Time Rock and Roll" on the stereo. He lip-synchs while dancing around the house in his underwear. These antics—which are refreshing in their manic energy and youthful exuberance—culminate in a gorgeous prostitute named Lana arriving at the house.

The relationship between Joel and Lana is the heart of the film. After they spend a romantic night together, he is shocked when she asks him to pay her three hundred dollars, which he doesn't have. Joel's problems escalate as Guido, Lana's pimp, becomes involved. In the meantime, Joel finds himself attracted to Lana while wishing she would go away so his life can return to normal before his parents come home. Still, despite the troubles caused by Lana, Joel seems the most honest and genuine when he's with her. They share quiet conversations in which they talk about their families and their futures. Later, when several of his family's possessions are stolen, he relies on Lana to help him sort out the mess that has spiraled way beyond his control.

In many ways, Lana provides Joel with more of an education than his own high school. She teaches him to be more savvy and confident in how he talks with other people, whether he's arguing with Guido, trying to impress the Princeton admissions officer in the midst of a raging party, or demanding that Lana and her girlfriend leave his house. Inadvertently, Lana also teaches him about responsibility. When he makes the mistake of leaving her alone in the house, he returns to discover that his mother's expensive glass egg has been stolen. Forced to deal with these issues on his own, Joel has to learn how to problem solve and make difficult decisions.

An important subtext in the film is capitalism. Joel and his friends are fascinated with making money. They talk about their ambitions as a way to conquer their fears. In one scene, they all sit in a restaurant and Joel asks if anyone wants to accomplish anything in life, or if they all just want to make money. There is a resounding agreement on making money. The film—with its focus on expensive cars, upper-class suburbs, and hip teenagers sporting Ray-Bans—suggests that, on some level, consumerism is a form of prostitution. Joel, while certainly not a hero, is a poster boy for materialism. And the film, though often funny, does not shy away from showing the consequences of his actions.

Why You Should See This Film: Because it's an insightful examination of the American dream and the pressures put upon teenagers to succeed in high school.

Main Themes: Guilt * Sexual Discovery * Responsibility * Teamwork * Deception

Classic Line: "I don't believe this! I've got a trig midterm tomorrow, and I'm being chased by Guido the killer pimp."

Recommended Double Feature: *The Diary of a Teenage Girl* (2015); Rated R, 102 minutes, Comedy-drama-romance

RUSHMORE

(1998)

Directed by: Wes Anderson
Written by: Wes Anderson and Owen Wilson
Cast: Jason Schwartzman (Max), Bill Murray (Herman), Olivia Williams (Rosemary)
Rating: Rated R for violence, adult content, and adult language
Runtime: 93 minutes
Genre: Comedy-drama

The Gist: Max Fischer is a fifteen-year-old student at Rushmore Academy, one of the best prep schools in the country. He possesses lofty ambitions, but he is also considered one of Rushmore's worst students. Part of Max's problem is that he spends little time studying. Instead, he focuses so much on extracurricular activities that he is in danger of flunking out. To inflate his sense of self-importance, Max immerses himself in all aspects of campus life. He is the president of the French Club, a member of the model United Nations, captain of the debate team, founder of the Astronomy Society, and vice president of the Stamp and Coin Club, just to name a few.

Max does display some admirable leadership qualities, but he is also a liar. He tells people his father is a doctor when he is really a barber. He also makes up several stories to appear tougher and cooler to his peers. Max acts like he belongs in the upper class, what with his poise and his vocabulary, but at home he eats TV dinners. Maybe this is why he is the

Jason Schwartzman, Olivia Williams. ***Buena Vista Pictures/Photofest © Buena Vista Pictures***

founder and director of the Max Fischer Players at Rushmore. They are a theater group that acts out plays Max has written, such as a version of the gritty cop drama *Serpico.*

The element of drama, and of playacting, is an important part of the film. The opening shot shows a painted portrait of a man, a woman, and two children. The man is Herman Blume, a millionaire in his forties who is as lonely as Max, though in different ways. The background of this opening shot is the red curtain we typically see on a stage. Following this opening shot, a blue curtain appears that opens up to reveal the film's title. The use of stage curtains to begin the film alludes to the crazy drama that will occur throughout, as well as the various performances that Max and Herman will put on to win the heart of Rosemary Cross, an elementary teacher with whom they have both fallen in love.

Herman Blume is a sad man. He's stuck in an unhappy marriage and annoyed with his two sons who are rude and obnoxious. While giving a speech at Rushmore, he offers the following advice to the students: "Take dead aim on the rich boys. Get them in the crosshairs and take them down. Just remember, they can buy anything but they can't buy backbone." This speech might seem strange coming from a millionaire, but Herman was not born rich. He earned his money by working hard, and this is what attracts Max to Herman. In speaking with Herman, Max understands that one doesn't need to come from money to be valuable and successful.

One day in the library, while reading *Diving for Sunken Treasure* by Jacques Cousteau, Max discovers a quotation scribbled in the margin. It centers on living an extraordinary life, and it sums up Max's beliefs about himself and his importance to Rushmore. He then takes it upon himself to find out who scribbled those poignant words. When Max learns that the book was donated to the library by Rosemary Cross, he falls in love with her.

Rosemary tells Max she is too old for him, but he doesn't care. His conversations with her expose his innocence and naïveté, but also his infatuation with a beautiful woman. His advances are equally comical and inappropriate. In a plan of epic proportion he decides to build an aquarium at Rushmore because he knows how much Rosemary likes fish. This detailed plan involves relocating the baseball diamond and Max getting into trouble with the school's administrators.

When Max meets with Herman to ask for start-up money, he introduces Herman to Rosemary. What results is a funny and vicious love triangle. Max and Herman attempt to win her over, the two of them acting like immature boys fighting on the playground. Their friendship quickly sours as they try to jeopardize the other man's chances. While their attempts to sabotage become increasingly violent, the mood is humorous given their deadpan delivery of the dialogue and their begrudging respect for each other's tenacity.

Despite the anger demonstrated by Max and Herman—as well as Rosemary's frustration with her persistent admirers—*Rushmore* is sweet and engaging in the way it makes us care about these two lonely people. The friendship between Max and Herman is the core of this story. The manner in which each of them helps the other to realize personal truths is funny and poignant. Both men are searching for a purpose in their life, and they're not above using sleazy tactics to find it.

Max writes and stages an original play toward the end of the film titled *Heaven and Hell.* It's a Vietnam War story complete with sound effects and explosions. Like everything else in his life, he prefers to go large so he can command attention and impress everyone. Max's title perfectly sums up the escalating conflict and drama in his life and in Herman's life. Both men embarrass themselves by grasping at love over and over again. They experience heartbreak and question their self-worth. But they are also interesting and likable. They just need to figure out how best to reveal it to the world without acting like selfish idiots.

Why You Should See This Film: Because it's a twisted and hilarious love story filled with immaturity and eccentricity.

Main Themes: Jealousy * Disillusionment * War * Love * Leadership

Classic Line: "I'm sorry, I just came by to thank you for WRECKING MY LIFE!"

Recommended Double Feature: *Moonrise Kingdom* (2012); Rated PG-13, 95 minutes, Drama-comedy

SAINT RALPH
(2004)

Directed by: Michael McGowan
Written by: Michael McGowan
Cast: Adam Butcher (Ralph), Gordon Pinsent (Father Fitzpatrick), Tamara Hope (Claire), Campbell Scott (Father Hibbert), Jennifer Tilly (Nurse Alice), Michael Kanev (Chester)
Rating: Rated PG-13 for some sexual content and partial nudity
Runtime: 98 minutes
Genre: Comedy-drama

The Gist: This film is based on the true story of a teenager named Ralph Walker who trained and competed in the 1954 Boston Marathon. Ralph attends a private Catholic school in Canada and lives by himself. His father has been killed in World War II and his mother is in the hospital, suffering from a serious illness. He visits her regularly to tell her about his life, but he exaggerates how well he is doing. She believes her son is staying with his friend Chester while she remains in the hospital. In the meantime, Ralph passes off forged notes to the school administrators that suggest his grandparents are taking care of him.

The film opens with Ralph in a confession booth, admitting to having impure thoughts and committing sins of the flesh. He thinks he's confessing to a priest, but his audience is actually a group of his classmates who then tease him. Ralph's sins, however, are natural for a teenager. He is lonely and interested in women, especially a fellow student named Claire whom he asks out in a touching and awkward scene. Though she seems interested, she cancels their date and tells Ralph she plans to become a nun.

Devoid of parental figures, Ralph attempts to act like a grown-up. He smokes cigarettes because it helps to calm his nerves, and he dresses up in his father's uniform. He is also mischievous and gets into trouble at school. In one scene, he spies on women changing inside the dressing room at the community pool. His excitement, coupled with a high-powered air jet, leads him to climax, which results in the pool being closed so it can be cleaned. These shenanigans, which include smoking on school grounds, result in Ralph being summoned to see the head priest, Father Fitzpatrick. He is a stern and emotionally distant man who questions whether Ralph is trying to purposefully get himself thrown out of school.

The film is a good mix of comedy and drama. The various tones reflect the constantly shifting moods experienced by adolescents. They highlight Ralph's immaturity, which is heightened by his father's death and his mother's absence. He is small and skinny and doesn't have any friends except for Chester, but he is a likable character. Ralph is selfless and caring, a bit of a sinner and a bit of a saint. And he's not afraid to stand up for what he wants or for what he believes.

Campbell Scott, Adam Butcher. *Samuel Goldwyn Films/Photofest © Samuel Goldwyn Films*

Frustrated with Ralph's deviant behavior, Father Fitzpatrick orders Ralph to attend six o'clock mass every morning and to join the cross-country team. The priest thinks engaging in these two activities will help to temper Ralph's physical and emotional energy. What he doesn't understand is that Ralph is trying the best he can to cope with his mother's illness. Ralph isn't receiving proper guidance and instruction away from school. And since Father Fitzpatrick believes Ralph needs to learn his place in the world, he chastises him instead of supporting him.

But then Ralph's mother slips into a coma. The doctors tell Ralph that only a miracle will wake her up. When he asks about miracles in class, another priest, Father Hibbert, tells him that, technically, anyone can produce a miracle. His words encourage Ralph to create his own miracle so he can save his mom. Later, after falling from the ropes in gym class, he has a vision in which God appears and tells him to run the Boston Marathon. Invigorated, Ralph now believes that winning the Boston Marathon will be the miracle his mother needs to awaken.

Unlike Father Fitzpatrick, Father Hibbert is warm and friendly. He teaches Nietzsche in his class and takes the time to talk honestly with his students. Because of his compassion, he has earned their respect. Father Hibbert coaches the cross-country team and eventually becomes Ralph's confidant. During the course of the film he also becomes a father figure to him. Despite pressure from Father Fitzpatrick for Ralph to not run the Boston Marathon, Father Hibbert stands up for Ralph and champions his pursuit of a miracle.

When Ralph announces his plan to run in the race, he is met with laughter and derision. But Ralph is an underdog who refuses to abandon his dream. He trains hard, practicing in all kinds of weather, and he learns how to run backward. He reads books that teach him how to control his breathing and build up his endurance. Even Nurse Alice, who tends to his mother, offers to lift weights with him. As Ralph trains harder and longer, he begins to earn the respect of his classmates. He also develops a sweet relationship with Claire, who likes Ralph and is impressed by his poise and determination.

The film moves along at a quick pace and contains such obligatory scenes as a training montage and the thrilling final sequence in which we root for Ralph to win the race. And while these clichés are well worn, they are wrapped up in the touching and uplifting story of an ordinary person who strives to accomplish an extraordinary feat.

Why You Should See This Film: Because it's a charming sports film that embraces the standard formula while transcending it with adolescent sensibilities.

Main Themes: Perseverance * Courage * Ambition * Grief * Authority

Classic Line: "Claire has clearly decided to put up the Great Wall of China defense on me. But I'm positive this whole nun thing is basically a way of denying her true feelings."

Recommended Double Feature: *Bend It Like Beckham* (2002); Rated PG-13, 112 minutes, Comedy-drama

SAY ANYTHING
(1989)

Directed by: Cameron Crowe
Written by: Cameron Crowe
Cast: John Cusack (Lloyd), Ione Skye (Diane), John Mahoney (James)
Rating: Rated PG-13 for adult content, adult language, and mild violence
Runtime: 100 minutes
Genre: Romantic comedy–drama

The Gist: This is a film that celebrates falling in love and taking risks. It's about two high school seniors named Lloyd Dobler and Diane Court who seem completely incompatible. Diane is the upper-class valedictorian who has been awarded a fellowship to study abroad in England. She lives with her father (James) who owns a retirement home. Lloyd, on the other hand, drives a beat-up car and lives with his sister, a single mother. His parents live in Germany because his father is in the army. Unlike Diane, Lloyd doesn't think about the future and has no idea what he'll do from one day to the next. But over the course of one tumultuous summer they both learn to care for and appreciate each other. In other words, it's an adolescent story filled with great music, classic one-liners, and realistic struggles.

The film begins at a high school graduation. This is a ceremony that symbolizes the beginning of adulthood for most teenagers. Yet, it also serves as the beginning of Lloyd and Diane's relationship. Feeling invigorated by receiving his diploma, Lloyd tells his friends he is going to ask her out. Of course, everyone thinks he is crazy and tries to convince him that it's a terrible idea. They fear he'll get his heart broken. But Lloyd shows a lot of courage when he locks himself in the bathroom to call her. He knows what he wants, and his determination is admirable. It's clear he would rather take a chance and be rejected than to not take a chance and always wonder what could have been.

Nervous and awkward, Lloyd invites Diane to a graduation party. Eventually, she accepts, though she doesn't seem too excited about their date. She feels uncomfortable around her classmates because they think she's a priss. In focusing solely on her education, in attending all the summer schools and in passing up fun vacations, she has sacrificed strong friendships. In this way, the film illustrates the importance of balancing personal time with academics. Diane is intelligent, but she separates herself from her classmates. In fact, we never see her confide in or hang out with a girlfriend during the course of the film. Diane's discomfort in social situations suggests that when it comes to maturity, establishing peer relations is just as important as earning good grades.

While at the party, Diane feels out of place. However, she relaxes as the party progresses, watching Lloyd interact with different groups of people as he collects keys from anyone who is too drunk to drive home. Their classmates are surprised that Diane came to the party, but also that she came with Lloyd. When they ask her why, she tells them he made her laugh. The graduation party is important because it allows Diane to go outside of her comfort zone. People are friendly and take the time to chat with her. She has a good time, which surprises her. She tells Lloyd she has never gone out with anyone as basic as he is, but she is attracted to his kind nature and how he acts like a gentleman.

As their relationship develops, they learn to trust each other. Diane, especially, learns to look past labels. Despite her father's disapproval, she wants to be with Lloyd and finds herself spending more time with him. He might not be as smart or as wealthy as she is, but he is not materialistic. He cares about who she is, and not about the accessories that define her. Diane's father, however, judges Lloyd based on his car and his appearance. He also doesn't like Lloyd's lack of vision. During a funny yet awkward dinner scene, Lloyd admits he doesn't know what he wants to do with his future, but he knows he wants to spend every moment with Diane. Concerned that his daughter will jeopardize her future, James pushes Diane to break up with Lloyd before she leaves for England at the end of the summer.

The film does a nice job of exploring the external conflicts that inform every relationship. Yes, Lloyd and Diane must deal with their own fluctuating emotions, but there are always outside factors that are beyond our control. For example, Diane has an open and honest relationship with her father, but he is also under criminal investigation by the IRS. This added stress, coupled with her father's dislike of Lloyd, causes friction among all three characters. These scenes are important because they show believable arguments between teenagers and their parents, especially in regard to whom they should date and how they should approach their future plans.

Lloyd is an appealing character because he feels like someone we all know. He is loyal, self-assured, thoughtful, and scared. At one point, he says, "I'm looking for a 'dare to be great' situation." It's precisely because of this confident attitude that he calls Diane and sets in motion a relationship so involving and nurturing that both of them are changed forever. And who can ever forget the iconic scene when Lloyd stands outside Diane's window, holding up his boom box to blare Peter Gabriel's song "In Your Eyes." It's a special moment filled with warmth and heartache that captures perfectly the dizzying emotions of being young and in love.

Why You Should See This Film: Because it's a funny and intelligent romance full of complex characters who try to be true to themselves while surrounded by doubt.

Main Themes: Insecurity * Class * Ambition * Honesty * Trust

Classic Line: "She gave me a pen. I gave her my heart and she gave me a pen."

Recommended Double Feature: *Love and Basketball* (2000); Rated PG-13, 124 minutes, Drama-romance

SCOTT PILGRIM VS. THE WORLD (2010)

Directed by: Edgar Wright

Written by: Edgar Wright and Michael Bacall, based on the graphic novel series *Scott Pilgrim* by Bryan Lee O'Malley

Cast: Michael Cera (Scott Pilgrim), Mary Elizabeth Winstead (Ramona Flowers), Kieran Culkin (Wallace Wells), Ellen Wong (Knives Chau)

Rating: Rated PG-13 for stylized violence, sexual content, language, and drug references

Runtime: 112 minutes

Genre: Action-fantasy

The Gist: Anyone who has ever played video games, especially the Nintendo 64 Classic in the 1980s, will appreciate *Scott Pilgrim vs. the World*. The main character, Scott Pilgrim, is a gangly twenty-two-year-old who lives in Toronto. He plays bass in an indie rock band called Sex Bob-Omb. Though he's dating a seventeen-year-old high school student named Knives Chau, Scott Pilgrim falls in love with Ramona Flowers. She's an American girl who delivers packages for Amazon. However, in order to win Ramona's love, Scott must first defeat Ramona's seven evil exes, including a vegan rock star, identical twins, and a famous actor/skateboarder.

The film is a mixture of fantasy and realism, full of eclectic music, and Japanese anime-style fight scenes. It assumes the look and feel of a video game. One of the pleasures is spotting homages to old-school classics like *Final Fantasy* and *Super Mario Brothers*, as well as watching kicks and punches that look like they've been lifted straight from *Street Fighter* and *Double Dragon*. Each of Ramona's evil exes functions as another game level that Scott must conquer in order to win Ramona's love, and each level becomes progressively more difficult. The fight scenes are chock full of the sorts of graphics and typefaces found in many video games. For example, the "demon hipster chicks" shoot fireballs, and the evil exes explode in a shower of coins whenever they're defeated.

Scott Pilgrim vs. the World presents a city populated by characters who are all in their teens and twenties. There are no parental figures to be seen or heard, and no disciplinarians to instruct the youth on matters of hygiene and etiquette. This absence of authority figures, coupled with the video-game-inspired action scenes, dilutes the film's realism and furthers the fantasy element. Any lecturing in *Scott Pilgrim vs. the World* is conducted by judgmental peers and concerned friends.

As a result, every character behaves as if he or she knows everything—acting haughty and disapproving, or laid back and sarcastic—when it's quite obvious that none of them has a firm grip on their own life. Instead of communicating openly, and considering the feelings of others, they're

Michael Cera, Mary Elizabeth Winstead. *Universal Pictures/Photofest* © *Universal Pictures*

trying to hold themselves together in the midst of petty insecurities and fractured relationships. They are driven forward by a need to be loved and showered with attention. In this way, Scott Pilgrim connects well with Ramona Flowers. While neither one is a teenager, both have stalled in their emotional development and now find themselves on a coming-of-age journey.

Scott and Ramona have difficulty reconciling their past mistakes, choosing instead to charge headlong into a future that seems so bright and dazzling. At the beginning of the film, Scott portrays an innocence and naïveté that defines him as a character who needs to be more active than passive. He doesn't want to grow up and assume adult responsibilities, a point made clear when the viewer realizes that he lives directly across the street from the house he grew up in. For him, the house symbolizes childhood comfort and security.

Scott Pilgrim just wants to rock out with his band and pretend that life is glorious and worry-free. This inexperience and gullibility is reflected in the film's manic energy—in the deft combination of rapid editing and witty dialogue—that suggests a brash and reckless abandon associated with youth. The picture explodes with colorful words and pictures. There is a flurry of pink and red hearts that float up when Scott and Ramona kiss. And when Knives tells Scott she's in love, the word "love" drifts out of her mouth in a beautiful pink cloud that Scott waves away as if it's secondhand smoke.

Scott Pilgrim vs. the World is satirical in the way it displays our childish attitudes toward love. The film shows how problems can arise when people treat a relationship like it's a game. The characters seek self-gratification because they want to be victorious, collecting points and gold coins because they believe that a relationship's worth is based on what they can show and not on what they can feel. And what the film also does is to show us that relationships can be as difficult and exhausting as a heroic quest fraught with peril.

Just like there are multiple levels in a video game, so are there multiple stages in every relationship. While an evil ex probably won't pick us up and throw us through a brick wall, there will always be challenges and obstacles that require our skills and attention. Sometimes, in a relationship we make bad decisions and have to use an "extra life." Sometimes, we have to consider which path to take and which items to carry with us because they're necessary for our survival. We all have emotional baggage, but the trick is to not let it weigh us down as we carry it forward day after day. Sometimes in life, we have to "level up," whether we want to or not.

Why You Should See This Film: Because it's a celebration of comic book energy laced with quirky dialogue and biting satire.

Main Themes: Apathy * Pretentiousness * Heroism * Communication * Jealousy

Classic Line: "When I'm around you, I kind of feel like I'm on drugs. Not that I do drugs. Unless you do drugs, in which case I do them all the time. Every drug."

Recommended Double Feature: *Youth in Revolt* (2009); Rated R, 90 minutes, Comedy-drama

SING STREET

(2016)

Directed by: John Carney
Written by: John Carney
Cast: Ferdia Walsh-Peelo (Conor), Lucy Boynton (Raphina), Jack Reynor (Brendan)
Rating: Rated PG-13 for strong language, sexual references, bullying behavior, and drug use
Runtime: 106 minutes
Genre: Comedy-drama

The Gist: *Sing Street* is a feel-good movie that makes you want to snap your fingers and pump your fists in the air. Set in Dublin in 1985, the film perfectly captures the look and atmosphere of the 1980s, from the fashions and hairstyles right down to the MTV videos. It's an absolute delight that celebrates the various ways that music can affect our lives, whether serving as an emotional escape from our daily problems or bringing us closer to those we care about.

The main character, Conor, is fourteen years old. He lives with his parents, older brother, and older sister in the inner city. His parents argue a lot and struggle financially. At the beginning of the film, they tell Conor they can't afford his expensive school and they're going to send him to Synge Street Christian Brothers School. But his first day doesn't go so well. He's bullied, mocked by his classmates, and told by the principal that he must follow the dress code and wear black shoes.

The only bright spot in Conor's day comes after school when he meets Raphina, an aspiring model. In order to impress her, he lies and tells her that he's a member of a band and needs a model to appear in one of their videos. Now, Conor must start a band. After convincing some of his classmates that joining a rock band will be a fun endeavor, the motley group practices weekly. They play cover songs of classic eighties groups like Duran Duran. Then, one day, Conor's brother (Brendan) tells him to quit covering other people's songs and, instead, to write his own music and lyrics.

This creative outlet suits Conor just fine. The music provides him with an outlet to express himself, not just for the depression he feels toward his home life and school life, but also for the attraction he feels toward Raphina. Conor, who looks up to Brendan, tells him how amazing and beautiful he finds Raphina. He explains that "she wears these sunglasses, and when she takes them off, her eyes are like the clouds clearing to let pass the moon." As Conor listens to different styles of music and shoots videos with Raphina and the band, he begins to acknowledge his true emotions and to write his own songs. In doing so, he becomes a more happy and confident person.

It's hard not to share in Conor's enthusiasm when he writes "Up" and "Riddle of the Model" for Raphina. Or when he stands onstage in his school auditorium and belts out "Drive It Like You Stole It," venting all of his frustrations. Conor delivers such catchy and upbeat songs that it's hard not to smile and appreciate the energy and enthusiasm that now propels him to make his own choices and to become an individual. The film shows how music can bring people together and provide a positive outlet for expressing themselves.

While music opens a new door into Conor's life, so does his relationship with Raphina. Experiencing love for the first time, he is shy and awkward until he allows his songs to speak for him. But love isn't always blissful, and Conor must learn to deal with the ups and downs of first kisses and false expectations. Raphina, who lives in an all-girls orphanage, has her own troubles and insecurities. She wants to move to London where she believes everything is bigger and better. Her life in Dublin seems lonely, but, like Conor and his bandmates, she seems to be at her happiest when she is surrounded by music.

Conor's budding relationship with Raphina allows him to better understand the arguments at home between his mother and father. His parents are on the verge of separating, and it is through music, listening to it and talking about it, that Conor bonds with his brother and sister, turning up the volume to drown out their parents' yelling. In this way, music helps him adapt to a strained home life, just as it helps him adapt to a new school and to a new love interest.

Sing Street champions the power of music to communicate. Yes, there are dramatic moments at home and at school, but the story, which is full of innocence and wonder, is heartening and inspiring. Music helps these characters to feel alive. It helps them adjust to the changes in their lives because it affords them power and a sense of purpose. As the film progresses, they become more distinct in how they dress and talk, asserting themselves as unique individuals.

At one point, Raphina tells Conor, "You can never do anything by half," and this advice is a good reminder that if we dream big, then we have to act big. The music Conor creates with the band gives him the motivation to face the obstacles in his life. Each song is a reflection of how he feels toward a world he is trying to understand. And in creating his own music and lyrics—in crafting an attitude toward certain people and certain events—Conor is figuring out who he is and who he wants to be.

Why You Should See This Film: Because it's an uplifting celebration of love, music, and family, all wrapped up in a collection of terrific songs.

Main Themes: Bullying * Authority * Family * Self-Awareness * Ambition

Classic Line: "Maybe you're living in my world. I'm not living in yours. You're just material for my songs."

Recommended Double Feature: *We Are the Best!* (2013); Not Rated, 102 minutes, Drama

SIXTEEN CANDLES
(1984)

Directed by: John Hughes
Written by: John Hughes
Cast: Molly Ringwald (Samantha), Anthony Michael Hall (The Geek), Michael Schoeffling (Jake), Gedde Watanabe (Long Duk Dong), Haviland Morris (Caroline)
Rating: Rated PG for language, brief nudity, and alcohol use
Runtime: 93 minutes
Genre: Romantic comedy

The Gist: The film takes place over the span of twenty-four chaotic hours in the life of a suburban high schooler named Samantha. It begins on the morning of her sixteenth birthday. While on the phone with a friend, she stands in front of her bedroom mirror, studying herself carefully to see if she has changed in any way. Sixteen is a pivotal age, and it's clear that Samantha wants to be seen more as an adult than as an adolescent. A birthday should be a joyous celebration with friends and family, but Samantha's entire day is about to become a total disaster.

Her older sister is getting married, and her entire family is preoccupied with the wedding preparations. Also, both sets of grandparents are staying at the house, as is a foreign exchange student named Long Duk Dong. As a result of the constant chaos—of everyone hurrying to eat breakfast and rushing out the door to go to school and work—Samantha's family completely forgets about her birthday. No presents. No cards. Not even a simple acknowledgment with a hug or a kiss.

Samantha, a sophomore, has a crush on a good-looking senior named Jake. But she's shy around him. She sneaks quick glances at him during class and then looks away whenever he catches her watching him. Jake is dating the gorgeous Caroline, though they don't seem very much in love. He seems disinterested while Caroline seems more interested with partying and maintaining her popularity. During an argument, Caroline reminds Jake there are lots of men who would kill to date her. Her statement suggests someone more concerned with power and control than with developing a mutual relationship. Their body language and tone also represent a couple that's about to crash and burn.

The problem, however, is that Jake and Samantha have never spoken to each other. Samantha wants Jake to notice her, but she isn't sure how to command his attention. But after filling out a sex quiz during class—in which Samantha admits she's a virgin and that she's saving herself for Jake—the quiz accidently ends up in Jake's hands. Though she didn't write her name on it, Samantha is still mortified. On the plus side, now that Jake realizes Samantha likes him, he decides to learn more about her. He begins asking people about her, which leads to an awkward but funny encounter at the school dance.

Then there's the Geek, a cocky but uncool freshman who flirts with Samantha on the bus. Later, at the school dance, he tries to romance her. The Geek bets his friends he can score with Samantha and assures them he'll bring back proof. His pursuit of Samantha results in the two of them sharing an honest and heartfelt scene in the auto shop that ends with him asking if he can borrow her underwear for ten minutes. The Geek is a major character in the film. His adventures throughout the night illustrate his immaturity, but they also show him as someone who is not as arrogant and self-centered as he seemed to be at the beginning of the film.

Long Duk Dong, the foreign exchange student, is one of the film's more interesting characters. Many people find his character offensive. He thinks American food is strange, speaks in broken English, and is used as a comic device. Every time he enters a scene, a gong sounds. Others have argued that Long Duk Dong does not adhere to the stereotype of remaining at home all the time to read and study. Instead of focusing solely on academics, he heads to the school dance and immediately finds romance. Later, he attends a raging party and gets drunk.

Sixteen Candles does a nice job of presenting characters that are familiar to us, but the film also humanizes them with unique characteristics. For example, Samantha doesn't throw a tantrum when her family forgets her birthday. She's hurt, but she doesn't whine or become vindictive. And while Jake is the popular guy with the beautiful girlfriend, he's sweet and caring. Even Samantha's father exhibits a nurturing tone when she confesses her attraction to Jake. He says, "That's why they call them crushes. If they were easy, they'd call them something else." His touching display of empathy is the response every adolescent hopes to receive from an adoring parent. Their late-night conversation validates her feelings and helps her to feel normal.

Though the film is rated PG, there is underage drinking and a brief shot of a woman's breasts. While these topics are often included in coming-of-age films, it's important to note that some of the content in the film is not representative of a PG rating. Still, this is one of the seminal teen films of the 1980s and should not be missed.

Why You Should See This Film: Because it's a sweet sixteen party that replaces cake and presents with family drama and blossoming love.

Main Themes: Perseverance * Acceptance * Trust * Pretentiousness * Insecurity

Classic Line: "I want a serious girlfriend. Somebody I can love, that's going to love me back. Is that psycho?"

Recommended Double Feature: *Never Been Kissed* (1999); Rated PG-13, 107 minutes, Comedy-drama

THE SPECTACULAR NOW
(2013)

Directed by: James Ponsoldt
Written by: Scott Neustadter and Michael H. Weber, based on the novel by Tim Tharp
Cast: Miles Teller (Sutter), Shailene Woodley (Aimee), Brie Larson (Cassidy), Kyle Chandler (Tommy), Jennifer Jason Leigh (Sara)
Rating: Rated R for alcohol use, language, and sexuality
Runtime: 95 minutes
Genre: Drama-romance

The Gist: This is a dramatic and heartwarming story centered on two teenagers who bond over the difficulties in their lives during their senior year of high school. Sutter is a smart and charismatic student who doesn't apply himself. He has no interest in what his future holds after he graduates. He cares about people and he has a big heart, but he's irresponsible. Sutter has a serious drinking problem too, and throughout the film he is seen sipping from either a flask or a container mixed with soda and alcohol. He also drinks and drives.

As the film begins, Sutter sits at his computer drinking a beer. He types a personal essay for a college application. The question he reads aloud is: "Describe a hardship, challenge or misfortune you have experienced in your life. What have you learned from this and how has it prepared you for the future?" The rest of the film is an answer to that question. As Sutter navigates through each day, he encounters numerous hardships and is forced to acknowledge his own issues. He explains that his girlfriend (Cassidy) dumped him the night before for one of the school's star athletes. He describes the two of them as being the life of every party, and because Sutter is upset he goes out drinking and passes out on someone's lawn.

He wakes up at six o'clock the next morning to find Aimee standing over him. They recognize each other from school, and Sutter offers to help her deliver newspapers. Aimee's father died of a drug overdose, and she lives with her mother, who is not dependable. She resents having to take care of her mother, and even comments that she probably won't go to college because her mother needs her. Sutter finds this unfair, but he bonds with Aimee because his home life is also chaotic. He lives with his mother too, and while she cares about him, she also works many hours at the hospital to support the family. Sutter's father is absent from his life, and his mother refuses to tell Sutter where he lives.

At school, Sutter is failing geometry because he doesn't study or turn in his homework. When his teacher asks him if he wants to graduate, Sutter shrugs and says he's not sure. He doesn't understand why he should want to become an adult. Basically, Sutter doesn't want to think about the future because then he will be forced to deal with his problems. While he prefers to live in the moment, Cassidy wants to plan for the future. But

Shailene Woodley, Miles Teller. *A24/Photofest © A24*

the future scares Sutter, so he lives in the present, which is predictable and stable. He shuts out everyone around him. Unlike other protagonists in coming-of-age films, however, Sutter is not afraid to admit that the real problem in his life is himself.

Sutter asks Aimee to tutor him, and their ensuing conversations reveal two people who need each other at this crucial point in their lives. When he tells her that she's a good listener, it's clear he isolates himself from people because he doesn't want to get emotionally attached. Therefore, it's touching when he becomes genuinely interested in Aimee and wants to know all about her. He even makes a point of telling his friend that Aimee is not a rebound relationship. Later, he invites her to a party and tries to boost her self-confidence by telling her she needs to start standing up for herself.

The revelations in *The Spectacular Now* are poignant because they occur naturally as a result of the characters' decisions. While at a dinner party, Aimee talks about her father's death and her idea of a perfect marriage. She says it's good to have dreams. Sutter, who likes being with Aimee, defends her by saying, "Once you've actually talked to her, you see who she is." Eventually, the two of them make a pact to stand up to their mothers, and when Aimee tells her mother she is going to attend college in Philadelphia, her accomplishment gives Sutter the courage to call his father and arrange a visit. He brings Aimee along for a day trip that proves to be exciting and disappointing, and which reveals secrets about his family he never knew.

When Sutter and Aimee do decide to have sex, it's one of the most awkward scenes in the film because it doesn't feel staged. Instead, it feels real, like two people who are discovering each other for the first time. They are clumsy and nervous, talking and laughing because they're not quite sure what will happen next. Their intimate moment is not necessarily romantic, but it is sweet and tender because it shows how much they care about each other. The scene is also important because it contains a wide range of honest emotions, all of which the characters display throughout the film as they learn to trust each other and to take chances. They understand that their futures don't have to be just a dream. If they work hard enough, and if they take responsibility for their own actions, then they can make those futures a reality.

Why You Should See This Film: Because it's a moving story about a reckless boy and an innocent girl trying to escape from their trapped lives.

Main Themes: Neglect * Fear * Communication * Guilt * Family

Classic Line: "It's fine to just live in the now. But the best part about now is that there's another one tomorrow. And I'm going to start making them count."

Recommended Double Feature: *The Fault in Our Stars* (2014); Rated PG-13, 133 minutes, Drama-romance

SPIDER-MAN: HOMECOMING
(2017)

Directed by: Jon Watts

Written by: Jonathan Goldstein, John Francis Daley, Jon Watts, Christopher Ford, Chris McKenna, and Erik Sommers

Cast: Tom Holland (Peter/Spider-Man), Michael Keaton (Adrian/Vulture), Marisa Tomei (May), Robert Downey Jr. (Tony Stark/Iron Man)

Rating: Rated PG-13 for sci-fi action, some language, and brief suggestive comments

Runtime: 133 minutes

Genre: Action-adventure

The Gist: The constant surprise of this film is how it deftly combines two popular genres, namely the superhero and the coming of age. Both genres center on physical and emotional ideas of power. They also center on the various ways that power can be wielded and controlled, whether positively or negatively. Each genre explores how possessing such power can affect our relationships with other people. Therefore, by placing a teenage protagonist inside a superhero film, the story is able to present the characters and the action as more than just thrilling entertainment. Instead, the hero's journey symbolizes the struggles inherent in growing up and becoming more independent.

Peter Parker is a nerdy fifteen-year-old who lives in New York City with his aunt May. He has few friends, and his idea of fun is building a Lego death star. At school, he finds it difficult to talk with girls. Peter is searching for a peer group he can join, a goal that's complicated by the fact that he spends a majority of his time alone because he has a secret identity. He is Spider-Man, the famous masked avenger who fights crime by swinging over crowded streets, and in between tall buildings, on a web that he shoots in all directions. While there have been several Spider-Man films over the years, this is the first to focus specifically on a high school version of Peter Parker, and to deal with adolescence as one of its main ideas.

During the opening minutes, Peter documents his first stint with the band of superheroes known as the Avengers. These moments make clear that this film will be fun and playful, presenting our hero as someone who's a bit immature. We see the home video footage Peter shot while being recruited by Tony Stark, and later we see him participating in his first mission. The tone is exciting and energetic, showing us a teenager who's thrilled to be included. Peter doesn't grasp the severity of his dangerous situation. Clearly, he likes being important and receiving attention from the public.

But back home in New York, Peter becomes impatient. He keeps waiting for Tony Stark to call him up and invite him on another mission. He quits marching band and robotics lab, rushing out of school as soon

Jacob Batalon, Tom Holland. *Columbia Pictures/Photofest © Columbia Pictures*

as the last bell rings so he can roam the city in search of crimes that need to be foiled. He wants to be productive and useful, but Tony Stark tells him to stay close to the ground. Peter becomes frustrated because he feels like Tony is treating him like a child. It also doesn't help that Peter can only access certain parts of his new Spidey suit, or that two of the suit's protocols are named Training Wheels and Baby Monitor.

The film's villain, referred to as the Vulture, is a man named Adrian Toomes. He initially owns a salvage company, but he begins stealing alien technology and manufacturing high-tech weapons when the government takes over his operation. As the Vulture, he flies through the air in a mechanical suit and is hell-bent on defeating Spider-Man. The reckless nature with which Spider-Man pursues the Vulture highlights his impulsivity and leads to several of the film's accomplished action scenes, particularly one at the Washington Monument and another that takes place on the Staten Island ferry. These scenes are loud and explosive, full of suspense and excitement. They are not simply set pieces plugged into the film, but key moments that expand on Peter Parker's character by illustrating his desires and limitations.

Here is a teenager so connected to his alter ego, so consumed with proving his self-worth, that he tells Tony Stark, "This is all I have. I'm nothing without this suit." Peter's subsequent journey toward self-discovery involves learning to be comfortable with himself as a teenager rather than as a superhero. He must learn to talk to girls without tripping over his own words. He must learn how to organize his time and juggle his responsibilities. And he must learn all of these things while butting heads with adult figures and trying to thwart the Vulture's diabolical plans.

What makes *Spider-Man: Homecoming* special are the ways in which typical coming-of-age moments weave themselves through the fabric of a superhero film. Typical arguments about safety and trustworthiness come from Aunt May and Tony Stark, who embody the mother and father characters. And Peter's suit comes equipped with its own artificial intelligence that he first refers to as "web suit lady" and then names Karen. In sharing his secrets with her, and in asking for relationship advice, the artificial intelligence symbolizes Peter's own conscience. In his search for important values like love and acceptance, Peter needs to remember that Spider-Man is only a part of him, and not all of him.

Why You Should See This Film: Because it's a superhero film that combines action and angst, highlighting the conflicts that arise while trying to attend high school, save the world, and crush on a cute girl.

Main Themes: Responsibility * Anger * Courage * Survival * Heroism

Classic Line: "Mr. Stark, here's my report for tonight. I stopped a grand theft bicycle. Oh, I helped this old lady and she bought me a churro. So, that was nice."

Recommended Double Feature: *Hanna* (2011); Rated PG-13, 111 minutes, Drama-action

STAND BY ME
(1986)

Directed by: Rob Reiner
Written by: Raynold Gideon, based on the novella "The Body" by Stephen King
Cast: Wil Wheaton (Gordie), River Phoenix (Chris), Corey Feldman (Teddy), Jerry O'Connell (Vern), Kiefer Sutherland (Ace)
Rating: Rated R for adult content and adult language
Runtime: 89 minutes
Genre: Drama

The Gist: The story takes place in the summer of 1959 and focuses on a group of twelve-year-old friends: Gordie, Vern, Chris, and Teddy. They leave their small town of Castle Rock, Oregon, to see the body of Ray Brower, a boy their own age who went to pick blueberries and disappeared. Their two-day trip, trekking across fields and walking over railroad tracks as they joke and make fun of each other, is not just a celebration of their friendship. It's also a nostalgic look at childhood, and at those pivotal times when we realize that the world is a lot larger than the narrow streets of our hometown.

Gordie is the main character. He's a budding writer, and when the film begins we see an older version of himself who reflects on those two fateful days when he and his friends set out across the countryside in search of the body. This older version of Gordie narrates the film, and his sentimental tone affords the film a depth and seriousness that blends well with the energy and innocence of the child characters. Like his three friends, Gordie's life is not without hardships. His older brother, Dennis, was killed in a jeep accident, and his parents are still finding it difficult to process the death. Living in his brother's shadow is tough, and Gordie feels like he's become invisible at home. His mother seems lost in her own world and barely looks at Gordie. His father, however, is always angry. He's still bitter over the loss of his favorite son, and he wonders aloud why Gordie can't have friends like Dennis.

But their lives change at the beginning of the film when Vern climbs up into the treehouse and asks his friends if they want to see a dead body. He then explains how he overheard a private conversation in which his brother and a friend talked about having discovered Ray Brower's body in the woods near the railroad tracks. So the four friends decide to pack their camping supplies and embark on an adventure.

Their journey takes them out of town, through a junkyard, and into the woods where they set up camp for the night. Gordie tells creative stories to his friends. They punch each other for flinching and engage in silly conversations, like debating which food they would eat for the rest of their lives if they could only choose one. They constantly rib each other

River Phoenix, Wil Wheaton. ***Columbia Pictures/Photofest © Columbia Pictures***

about weight and intelligence, and they make fun of each other's mothers. All of this is done in a juvenile way that's not mean spirited, but which reveals their youth and naïveté.

There are serious moments too. Like when Gordie asks Chris if he thinks he's weird. And Chris, who cares a lot about Gordie, says yes, but that it doesn't matter because everyone's weird. Or when Chris admits to Gordie that he's worried the four friends will split up once they begin middle school. He's worried that Gordie will make new friends because he's smart and will probably take college-level classes. Then there's Teddy, who's been abused by his father, but still becomes emotional when a man insults his father by calling him a loony.

The film is also bittersweet. These four friends don't want their special moments to end—mostly because they rely on each other for support—so they're making the most of their time together now. While their close friendship helps them to deal with the numerous problems in their lives, there's a strong sense that each of them is heading in a different direction. The future scares all of them, whether they're discussing school or potential jobs or their dysfunctional families. In completing this dangerous journey, they hope to form a bond that will last forever, no matter how distant they might become.

A subplot in the film involves a gang of older teens, led by a hoodlum named Ace. He and his friends smash mailboxes and threaten people with switchblades. They also want to find Ray Brower, which puts them on a collision course with Gordie and his friends. Both groups are fascinated with the idea of seeing a dead body. They aren't repulsed by death. On the contrary, they're deeply interested in it, as if they haven't yet grasped a sense of their own mortality. Ray Brower's body, then, becomes a symbol for the darker aspects of life, for those crucial moments that allow us to understand the world better and to learn from it.

Stand by Me is a film about boundaries, both physically and emotionally. And it's about the importance of crossing those boundaries. At one point Chris tells Gordie, "Kids lose everything unless there's someone there to look out for them." These four childhood friends are as important to one another as family. They laugh and cry together, they stand up for each other, and they share their fears with honesty. In this way, their adventure becomes much more than just a long hike through the woods to see a dead body.

Why You Should See This Film: Because it's about four inseparable and vulnerable friends who lose their innocence while trying to figure out what's important in their lives.

Main Themes: Friendship * Death * Family * Neglect * Empathy

Classic Line: "Everything was there and around us. We knew exactly who we were and exactly where we were going. It was grand."

Recommended Double Feature: *Flipped* (2010); Rated PG, 90 minutes, Drama

SUBMARINE
(2010)

Directed by: Richard Ayoade
Written by: Richard Ayoade, based on the novel by Joe Dunthorne
Cast: Craig Roberts (Oliver), Yasmin Paige (Jordana), Paddy Considine (Graham), Noah Taylor (Lloyd), Sally Hawkins (Jill)
Rating: Rated R for language and sexual content
Runtime: 97 minutes
Genre: Comedy-drama-romance

The Gist: Set in Swansea, Wales, this quirky and twisted story centers on fifteen-year-old Oliver Tate, a contemplative young man who lives with his mother and father. He carries a briefcase to school and reads the dictionary for fun. He's a loner who prefers spending time with himself because it gives him time to think. At school, Oliver wonders how people would react to his death, imagining candlelit vigils and sobbing girls. His fantasies inflate his sense of self-importance because they're an escape from the bullying he sometimes endures. Yet amid his daily struggles, Oliver makes it his mission to accomplish two important goals before his next birthday. One is to lose his virginity, and the other is to save his parents' crumbling marriage.

The film is structured like a novel. There's a prologue, three parts, and an epilogue. Oliver's voice-over informs us of how he feels about critical moments in his life, and of how he would like certain situations to play out. During the opening scene, for example, Oliver states, "Most people think of themselves as individuals, that there's no one else on the planet like them." This idea of individualism is explored throughout the film in conflicting ways. For example, Oliver clearly struggles to form his own self-identity—in the way he dresses and speaks—but he is also a social outcast who wants to fit in so badly that at times he participates in bullying other students.

Oliver's world is turned upside down when he develops a crush on Jordana. He finds her mysterious and lovely. The only flaw he notices are her sporadic outbursts of eczema. Jordana possesses a bullying streak herself and actually uses Oliver to make her ex-boyfriend jealous. Jordana also has intimacy issues and finds it difficult to express herself to others. But she enjoys spending time with Oliver. Together, the two of them take long walks along the beach and find common ground in being alienated by their peers. Oliver tries to impress Jordana by speaking philosophically about his own emotions and his unique views on life. And there's a funny scene where he attempts to romance her with red balloons, candles, and mood lighting.

Oliver's behavior is not surprising when one considers that his parents are just as odd as he is. His mother, Jill, is neurotic and thinks Oliver has mental problems. She worries about his introversion and often catches him spying on her. When he tells her he has a girlfriend, she doesn't believe him at first. His father, Lloyd, is a marine biologist who suffers from depression. Upon learning about Oliver's girlfriend, his father gives him a mixtape of relationship songs, including some that focus on heartache just in case they break up.

Added to Oliver's relationship anxiety is the fact that his parents are experiencing marital problems. The cause of their tension is the recent arrival of a man named Graham who moves in next door. Graham was his mother's first love. He's a new-age, self-help guru with a live show that advertises "psychic and physical excellence." Oliver refers to him as "the ninja" on account of Graham's fondness for executing jabs and kicks at random moments. Graham sports a ridiculous mullet and is flirtatious with Jill to the point that Oliver is convinced his mom is having an affair with Graham.

The film does a nice job of showing the pains of first love. Oliver stammers a lot and finds himself second-guessing important decisions. He tries talking to his parents about their problems, leaving notes around the house and lecturing to them in a stern voice. But in attempting to act like a grown-up, it's clear that Oliver lacks both understanding and an adult perspective. When Jordana reveals that she is experiencing problems in her own home life, Oliver struggles with how to handle his girlfriend and his parents at the same time. Because he doesn't know how to comfort Jordana, he feels awkward and begins to withdraw, which causes a rift in their relationship.

The film's title comes from the idea of feeling so depressed that it seems as if you're trapped on the bottom of the ocean. Multiple characters exhibit sadness and regret throughout the film. Oliver's observations of the people around him provide a lesson that if he wants to form adult relationships, then he will have to learn how to deal with adult problems. How Oliver deals with those issues is touching, funny, and sad, sometimes all at the same time. He envisions his life as a film, and he wishes there was a crew to follow him around all day long. This fantasy, in which his life is defined by camera angles and a brilliant soundtrack, illustrates his desire to be a profound person who performs meaningful actions that are worthy of everyone's attention and admiration.

Why You Should See This Film: Because it's a sweet and funny exploration of love that isn't afraid to venture into absurdity.

Main Themes: Bullying * Death * Communication * Sexual Discovery * Depression

Classic Line: "I don't quite know what I am yet. I've tried flipping coins, listening exclusively to French crooners. . . . I've even had a brief hat phase, but nothing stuck."

Recommended Double Feature: *Spud* (2010); Not Rated, 103 minutes, Comedy

SUPERBAD

(2007)

Directed by: Greg Mottola
Written by: Seth Rogen and Evan Goldberg
Cast: Michael Cera (Evan), Jonah Hill (Seth), Emma Stone (Jules), Christopher Mintz-Plasse (Fogell), Martha MacIsaac (Becca), Seth Rogen (Officer Michaels), Bill Hader (Officer Slater)
Rating: Rated R for alcohol and drug use, crude and sexual content, and strong language
Runtime: 113 minutes
Genre: Comedy

The Gist: This film is the perfect blend of vulgarity and sweetness. It takes place over the span of twenty-four hours and focuses on two high school seniors named Seth and Evan. They have been best friends since childhood and are preparing to attend different colleges. Neither one is popular at school, especially Seth because he is overweight. A bully spits on Seth as he and Evan leave a convenience store; later, someone knocks his textbooks off the cafeteria table. As with many adolescent boys, their conversations revolve around sex and drinking. Their language is often crude, but it's also quite colorful and creative. They use their words to sound intelligent and confident, but it's clear they are inexperienced and unsure of themselves.

Seth and Evan constantly hang out with each other, and their relationship appears to be codependent. Evan's mother alludes to this at the beginning of the film when she wonders how the two of them will function next year when they are apart from each other. Both of them also find it difficult to flirt with girls. Seth has a crush on Jules, and Evan likes Becca. Their interactions with both girls provide some of the film's funnier moments. Seth leans toward crude language in his nervousness while Evan's shyness creates several awkward situations.

Their luck improves, however, when they are both invited to a party that Jules is throwing while her parents are out of town. Wanting to impress her, Seth brags about being able to buy alcohol, which prompts Jules to give him one hundred dollars and ask if he'll buy alcohol. Becca, meanwhile, asks Evan to buy her a bottle of vodka. For both adolescents, this sudden attention is a milestone event they don't want to waste. Seth tells Evan they need to take advantage of their last party as high schoolers. Feeling like they haven't capitalized on the past four years, they want to look cool in front of their peers.

Seth and Evan solicit the help of their friend Fogell, who has just purchased a fake ID. Like his friends, Fogell is unpopular. When Seth and Evan look at his fake ID, they freak out because he chose the name "McLovin." Annoyed, they rip into him for choosing a stupid name, but then realize they depend on Fogell and his fake ID if they want to purchase

Jonah Hill, Michael Cera. ***Columbia Pictures/Photofest © Columbia Pictures. Photographer: Melissa Moseley***

alcohol and impress the girls. Purchasing alcohol and getting to the party prove much more difficult than any of them could have imagined. Once inseparable, the three friends are split apart by a series of hilarious circumstances. Fogell's attempt to purchase booze ends with him being a witness to a robbery and riding around with two hilarious and lazy police officers.

In the midst of the crass conversations and the crazy hijinks, several conflicts rise to the surface. Seth is shocked when he learns that Evan is bringing a condom and a little bottle of spermicidal lube to the party. Seth is upset that he wasn't told about this plan, and his frustration illustrates his dependency on Evan. His outburst also reveals a deeper issue, mainly that Seth is mad because Evan will attend Dartmouth. Seth always thought the two of them would go to college together, and he's afraid their friendship will deteriorate. In a brief moment of anger, Evan yells, "I'm not going to let you slow me down anymore, Seth." This scene, which is honest but uncomfortable, shows that they both understand the fact that change is inevitable. No matter what happens after they graduate, their relationship will change to some degree.

The stress of graduating high school and leaving for college is evident in the characters' actions and conversations, which show they still need to mature before leaving home. Seth and Evan run from the police, consider stealing alcohol, and claim to be ready for sexual activity when it's clear they have no clue what it means to be passionate. Toward the end of the film, when Evan is making out with a girl, she tells him she's becoming aroused. His response is that he knew that would happen because he learned about it in his health class.

While the language in *Superbad* might be too strong for some viewers, it's not simply used for shock effect. Instead, it masks the characters' insecurities and reveals their ignorance. When Evan tells Seth that everyone has sex in college, it illustrates their foolish idea that college is one big party where they won't have to work hard to secure a romantic relationship. They want desperately to enter the adult world so they don't have to be dorky teenagers anymore. The dialogue exposes them as timid and apprehensive. More importantly, it shows them as realistic teenagers who are eager to move on to the next phase of their lives while still trying to claim the glory that's escaped them during the high school years.

Why You Should See This Film: Because it's a raunchy yet tender story of two best friends and their pursuit of girls and alcohol during one last high school party.

Main Themes: Sexual Discovery * Friendship * Selfishness * Jealousy * Courage

Classic Line: "I still think you have a chance with Jules. She got incredibly hot over the summer, and she obviously hasn't realized it yet because she's still always talking to you and flirting with you and stuff."

Recommended Double Feature: *Blockers* (2018); Rated R, 102 minutes, Comedy

TO ALL THE BOYS I'VE LOVED BEFORE
(2018)

Directed by: Susan Johnson
Written by: Sofia Alvarez, based on the novel by Jenny Han
Cast: Lana Condor (Lara Jean), Noah Centineo (Peter), Israel Broussard (Josh), John Corbett (Dr. Covey), Anna Cathcart (Kitty), Janel Parrish (Margot), Emilija Baranac (Genevieve)
Rating: Rated TV-14 for teen romance
Runtime: 99 minutes
Genre: Romantic comedy

The Gist: Lara Jean is a quiet sixteen-year-old beginning her junior year of high school. She lives a comfortable life in Portland, Oregon, with her father (Dr. Covey) and two sisters. They are a close family and still mourning the loss of their mother. Lara Jean is the middle child. Her younger sister (Kitty) is an intelligent and energetic sixth grader. Her older sister (Margot) is leaving home to attend a university in Scotland. Their father, a gynecologist, is a fun and easygoing man who's built a loving and trusting relationship with his three daughters.

The film's opening credits show Lara Jean walking through a lush green field in a beautiful red dress. She is walking toward an attractive boy. As she does so, her voice-over talks about an illicit love and the power of fate. The atmosphere is so dreamy that it seems like the entire scene has been pulled from the pages of a romance novel. The film then cuts to Lara Jean's bedroom where she is actually reading a book titled *The Forbidden*

Kiss. She has been fantasizing about her most recent crush, who happens to be her next-door neighbor, Josh. He is also Margot's boyfriend whom her sister has been dating for the past two years.

However, Lara Jean is not trying to steal Josh from Margot. He's one of her closest friends, and she doesn't want to jeopardize their closeness. Despite being smart and pretty, Lara Jean doesn't have a boyfriend, and she has no interest in acquiring one. While she loves to read novels in which characters date and fall in love, she finds it scary to imagine herself in an intimate relationship. She would much rather fabricate the perfect version of someone in her mind rather than be with a real person.

Because Lara Jean is reluctant to act on her emotions, she wrote Josh a letter to express how she felt about him. She sealed it in an envelope and addressed it, but she never mailed it. Instead, she now keeps this letter in a box in her closet. She has written four other letters, too, each one addressed to a different boy. She says, "I write a letter when I have a crush so intense that I don't know what else to do." Lara Jean's five letters are her most secret possessions. They remind her how powerful her own emotions can be. But in keeping them hidden away in her closet, she essentially buries her own feelings and desires.

At school, Lara Jean is neither popular nor unpopular. She is simply invisible, which seems to suit her just fine. Kitty, however, is worried about her. One Saturday night, while the two of them are at home, Kitty tells Lara Jean that she canceled plans to be with her older sister. She also wishes her sister would date someone. These heartfelt conversations show how much the sisters care about one another. They also illustrate Lara Jean's introversion. Still reeling from the loss of her mother, she is afraid of letting anyone into her life because there is always the possibility that person will leave. She needs to learn that to love someone is to take risks.

Noah Centineo, Lana Condor. *Netflix/Photofest* © *Netflix*

But then, somehow, all five of Lara Jean's letters are mailed out to each of her crushes. Naturally, chaos ensues. One of the recipients, Peter, has just broken up with his girlfriend, Genevieve. She is Lara Jean's former best friend from middle school. She is also stuck up and mean. After confronting Lara Jean about his letter, Peter suggests the two of them pretend to be a couple. He wants to make Genevieve jealous in the hope that she'll want to renew their relationship. Although hesitant at first, Lara Jean soon agrees to the idea and insists they draw up a contract. The contract they sign contains such stipulations as no kissing, the passing of handwritten notes each day, and a mandatory viewing of *Sixteen Candles*.

Lara Jean is used to wandering around the high school unnoticed, but when she starts "dating" Peter, all of her classmates begin to look at her and talk about her. She eats with him in the cafeteria and becomes friends with his friends. People tell Lara Jean they've never seen her so happy. Even her father mentions how proud he is that she's dating a nice boy and going to parties. While many coming-of-age films illustrate the negative side of an adolescent's social life, this one shows how it can lead to self-reflection and emotional growth.

The fake relationship that Lara Jean and Peter create turns out to be more real than either of them expected. Of course, they develop strong feelings for each other, which further complicates their contract. But the time they spend together teaches them how to be more honest with themselves and with each other. Lara Jean is afraid to share her secret feelings because she knows that doing so makes her vulnerable to being hurt by someone she cares about. Eventually, though, she realizes that love is only forbidden if we never take a chance on it.

Why You Should See This Film: Because it's a sweet and upbeat story about two people venturing outside their comfort zones to find happiness.

Main Themes: Honesty * Communication * Self-Confidence * Acceptance * Courage

Classic Line: "The more people that you let into your life, the more that can just walk right out."

Recommended Double Feature: *Candy Jar* (2018); Rated TV-14, 92 minutes, Comedy-romance-drama

VALLEY GIRL
(1983)

Directed by: Martha Coolidge
Written by: Andrew Lane and Wayne Crawford
Cast: Nicolas Cage (Randy), Deborah Foreman (Julie), Michael Bowen (Tommy), Colleen Camp (Sarah), Frederic Forrest (Steve), Cameron Dye (Fred)
Rating: Rated R for profanity, sexual language, nudity, and drug use
Runtime: 99 minutes
Genre: Romantic comedy

The Gist: Julie and Randy are two high school kids from different parts of town. She attends Valley High. He attends Hollywood High. Her friends are upper class and snobby, whereas his are middle class and humble. Despite these glaring differences, or perhaps because of them, the two end up falling in love. Filled with eighties music and, like, totally bitchin' slang, this is a funny and updated version of Shakespeare's *Romeo and Juliet*. Instead of the families that disapprove, though, it turns out to be Julie's friends.

The beginning of the film shows us life in the valley as Julie and her girlfriends shop at the mall. They model clothes and shoes and bracelets, charging hundreds of dollars on their credit cards. Later, they sit in the food court at the mall and talk about boys and parties. Julie is unhappy with her boyfriend, Tommy. She tells her friends that he's really cute but not very smart. Tommy is a selfish jerk who doesn't call Julie or act like he even cares about her. He's concerned with his own image and wants every girl to obsess over him. Julie, however, is bored with the relationship, so she dumps him.

Later, at the beach, Julie spots Randy and is instantly attracted to him. She and her girlfriends stare at him and call him a hunk, commenting on his pecs. Because Randy is only wearing a bathing suit, he is dressed exactly like everyone else. Without designer labels to characterize him, the focus is simply on what he looks like. There is an interesting sense of equality at the beach, but it disappears as soon as everyone changes out of their bathing suits and into more defining clothes. At the beach, they are judging each other's bodies on a purely emotional level; in the community, they are judging each other's fashion choices.

However, the conflict is set in motion when Randy is told of a party that night and says he doesn't want to go into the valley. It's clear that he and his friends from the city don't mesh well with Julie and her friends. These differences are illustrated in hilarious detail at the party that night when the parents serve homemade sushi. This unique food choice for a teenage party highlights the importance that money and sophistication play in the lives of the valley kids and their parents. Consequently, when Randy and Fred show up, they are stared at by everyone in the house, not least because they look like punks while the valley dudes wear button-up shirts.

Randy and Julie spot each other from across the room and begin a conversation. When Tommy sees Julie flirting with another guy, however, he and his friends throw Randy and Fred out of the house. They leave, but Randy decides to sneak back inside so he can talk more with Julie. The love story that develops is sweet and funny, but realistic in its depictions of how our feelings can be influenced and shaped by our friends and family. Julie admits that her friends will freak out when they discover she's dating Randy because he doesn't talk or dress like anyone at Valley High. And they keep pressuring her to get back together with Tommy, not because he's a decent guy, but because he's handsome and popular.

Then there are Julie's parents, who are nurturing and supportive. They're hippies who smoke pot and own a health food store. They allow Julie the freedom to make her own decisions and to be independent. Her mom admits that they give Julie as much space as she needs. Their stance on letting her grow up is different from her friends who want her to make decisions based on her popularity. Her friends are selfish because they want Julie's personal decisions to make them appear cool too. They're more concerned with what *looks* right than with what *is* right.

Julie is torn between Randy and Tommy, and it's obvious that her friends are influencing her in a negative way. In one of the film's more tender moments, Julie sits at home with her father and ask him for advice. He says, "There are lots of people out there who just aren't happy unless you live and think the same way they do." This echoes a strong message in the film, namely that it's important to be an individual and to think for ourselves. Her father preaches the idea that it's not only okay to be different, but it's expected because it's our differences that make us special.

The film applauds these ideas through Julie and Randy's developing relationship. And Randy—though he's viewed by Julie's friends as stupid and uncultured—offers some of the most poignant remarks in the film. He understands that Julie's friends are prejudiced and immature, and that they're focused more on material desires than personal ones. But he demonstrates admirable determination by refusing to let Julie walk out of his life.

Valley Girl doesn't fault Julie for her confusion. She's young and just beginning to understand that sometimes love can be baffling and frustrating. The audience knows she should be with Randy, but we still understand the conflicts she experiences while trying to figure out what she should do and how she should do it. And that celebrated final shot is just a perfect blend of hope, uncertainty, and unlimited possibilities of what the future holds.

Why You Should See This Film: Because it's, like, a totally awesome flick about being in love and staying true to yourself.

Main Themes: Pretentiousness * Judgment * Perseverance * Class * Peer Pressure

Classic Line: "Hi, I'm Fred. I like tacos and '71 Cabernet. My favorite color is magenta."

Recommended Double Feature: *Grease* (1978); Rated PG-13, 111 minutes, Musical-comedy-romance

THE WAY WAY BACK
(2013)

Directed by: Nat Faxon and Jim Rash
Written by: Nat Faxon and Jim Rash
Cast: Liam James (Duncan), Toni Collette (Pam), Steve Carell (Trent), Sam Rockwell (Owen), AnnaSophia Robb (Susanna), Zoe Levin (Steph)
Rating: Rated PG-13 for thematic elements, language, some sexual content, and brief drug material
Runtime: 103 minutes
Genre: Comedy-drama

The Gist: Here is a film so sweet and charming that it's difficult not to like. It's a feel-good story about a fourteen-year-old introvert named Duncan who learns how to talk to people and to stand up for himself. Yes, it contains the usual offerings of tongue-tied romance and strained family dynamics, but it's also a funny and realistic look at adolescence. Set amid the backdrop of beautiful beaches, backyard barbecues, and crowded water parks, the film takes place during one tumultuous summer.

Duncan is shy and awkward, and he keeps to himself. In fact, he's happy to not do much of anything. It's his vacation, and he wants to spend it with his father who lives in San Diego. Instead, he's forced to travel with his mom (Pam) and her boyfriend (Trent) to a seaside town in Massachusetts where they stay at Trent's beach house. Along for the ride is Trent's spoiled and stuck-up daughter, Steph, who either ignores Dun-

AnnaSophia Robb, Liam James. ***Fox Searchlight Pictures/Photofest © Fox Searchlight Pictures***

can or treats him like he's a complete loser. While all the neighbors hang out and party—singing and dancing, grilling, and telling jokes—Duncan hides in the shadows, looking depressed. He sits on the beach alone because he doesn't like Trent.

Trent is rude and overbearing. He continuously says he wants the four of them to be a family, but it's clear he doesn't respect Duncan. Whenever Trent attempts to make a personal connection with him, he just ends up condescending Duncan as if he is five years old. In the opening scene, for instance, Trent asks him how he would rate himself on a scale of one to ten. Duncan is uncomfortable with the conversation, only answering when Trent prods him. While he rates himself a six, it's obvious that Duncan has no opinion because he doesn't see himself in any particular way. However, he is even more embarrassed when Trent disagrees and calls him a three. Later, when everyone goes boating, Trent makes Duncan wear a life preserver, which isolates him even more because no one else is wearing one.

Needing to flee the house, Duncan finds a girl's bicycle in the garage and pedals around to explore the town. Eventually, he finds himself at Water Wizz, the local water park run by Owen. Unlike Trent, Owen is a laid-back beach bum who enjoys kidding around and not worrying. He hires Duncan to perform random jobs around the water park. The job not only affords Duncan a sense of responsibility, but it forces him to be part of a community that acknowledges and appreciates him. Through his time at Water Wizz, Duncan learns how to express his feelings and to process the drama unfolding back at the beach house.

One of the most rewarding friendships that Duncan enjoys is with the attractive Susanna. She lives in the house next door with her mother and younger brother, and though she hangs out with Steph sometimes, she doesn't seem interested in being part of that social circle. The initial conversations between Susanna and Duncan are short and uneasy, including a moment when she catches him singing "Can't Fight This Feeling" while lying on top of Trent's car. Eventually, the two of them take walks along the beach and confide in each other. They bond over their fractured families. As Duncan's self-confidence grows at Water Wizz, he becomes more vocal and assertive at the beach house, standing up not only for himself, but also for his mother.

What's interesting about *The Way Way Back* is how the adult conflicts are just as interesting as the adolescent ones. In fact, the adults in the film often act like teenagers themselves, giggling and making fun of each other while drinking and smoking pot. True, they're unwinding on vacation, but there is a lack of maturity and compassion in the way they treat each other. Duncan doesn't like that his mother neglects him by spending more time with Trent. Nor does he appreciate it when Trent tells him they need to develop trust and respect to make their family unit work, but then lies to Pam and belittles her.

The film's title is a reference to the very back of the car, which is exactly where Duncan sits whenever the family goes for a ride. Being banished to the way way back—isolated in a cramped space while looking back and not ahead— symbolizes how the adults don't accept him or take him seriously. As well, sitting in the way way back highlights the emotional distance Duncan creates between himself and everyone else. He's living off limited experiences, and like any teenager he needs to learn that there is a bigger world out there.

At the core of the film is the relationship between Duncan and Owen. In one of the more poignant scenes, Owen tells him, "You gotta go your own way. And you, my friend, are going your own way." He provides

Duncan with much-needed guidance, and he does so in a positive atmosphere where Duncan can separate himself from the hurt and anger he feels at home. Owen doesn't judge Duncan either. Instead, he recognizes his potential and helps him to unleash it.

Why You Should See This Film: Because it's a funny film with a big heart, showing the pains and joys of adolescence as they vie for attention in the hot summer sun.

Main Themes: Insecurity * Neglect * Responsibility * Authority * Family

Classic Line: "I'm afraid I'm going to have to ask you to leave. We're getting complaints. You're having way too much fun. It's making everyone uncomfortable."

Recommended Double Feature: *The Kings of Summer* (2013); Rated R, 96 minutes, Drama-adventure

WELCOME TO THE DOLLHOUSE
(1995)

Directed by: Todd Solondz
Written by: Todd Solondz
Cast: Heather Matarazzo (Dawn), Matthew Faber (Mark), Daria Kalinina (Missy), Brendan Sexton III (Brandon), Eric Mabius (Steve)
Rating: Rated R for language
Runtime: 88 minutes
Genre: Black comedy–drama

The Gist: Dawn Wiener is the middle child in a family that consists of a brainy older brother (Mark), a beautiful younger sister (Missy), and parents who don't seem to pay her much attention. Her school life is equally miserable, as she is shy and unpopular. She is taunted by her classmates and called names like "Wiener Dog" and "Lesbo." Students write all over and around Dawn's locker, marking her as an outcast. When she asks one girl why she hates her so much, the girl tells Dawn it's because she's ugly.

At the beginning of the film, Dawn stands in the cafeteria, clutching her lunch tray and looking for someplace to sit. The awkwardness of this scene—her apparent loneliness and the disgusted glances she receives from her classmates—sets the tone for this bleak yet funny film in which Dawn deals with her annoying family, lusts after a high school boy who plays in her brother's band, and develops a strange relationship with a bully who torments her at school.

The film is quirky in its characters and their behaviors, which are often unexpected. Missy wears a ballerina outfit and twirls around like a cute little girl. But she is not above tattling on Dawn and getting her into trouble. Mark is only concerned with getting into a good college and repeatedly mentions his college resume; a poster of Einstein hangs in his bedroom, and he seems more concerned with grades than with maintaining a long-distance relationship with his girlfriend. And Brandon, the bully who threatens to rape Dawn after school, shows a sensitive side when he talks about his brother who is developmentally challenged; later, he engages Dawn in several honest conversations.

And Dawn is just as unpredictable. She feels hurt and scared at school when the other students bully her, but when she returns home she transfers that anger to Missy. For example, when girls in the lunchroom call Dawn a lesbo, she calls Missy a lesbo at home and gets into trouble. When Brandon mouths profanity to her in class, Dawn then mouths profanity to Missy at the dinner table. And in one of the film's funniest displays of aggression, Dawn sits on her bed and saws the head off of Missy's Barbie doll. These scenes are realistic in showing how we often release our anger by directing it at other people. We command the power and control we desperately want to cling to, especially during our formative years as we become more independent.

What makes these characters so interesting is that all of them are humanized. There are moments when we dislike them and moments when we empathize with them. It appears that Brandon wants to sexually assault Dawn, but his intimidation reveals an interest in her on a romantic level. Likewise, we understand the jealousy Dawn feels toward Missy, but the malice Dawn displays at home illustrates the resentment she feels toward her entire family. Dawn even admits she wants to be popular, which is why she has a clubhouse in her backyard called the Special People Club. The Special People Club is her escape, a fantasyland where she can be liked for who she is and where she can be assured of her self-worth.

Dawn experiences a lot of conflict and stress in her life, but she still finds time to pursue Steve Rodgers, a handsome and popular high schooler who plays guitar and sings. The moments centered on Dawn's infatuation with Steve are simultaneously hilarious and awkward. Her attempts at flirting involve offering to make him Jell-O, watching band practice while executing some dance moves, and asking him if he wants to join her Special People Club. In one scene, after stealing his license, Dawn lights some candles and creates a shrine for her crush, chanting, "Steve, Steve, Steve. Hear me. You will fall in love with me. You will make love to me. You will take me away from this place." The hopefulness and innocence that Dawn exhibits during these scenes reveal that Steve Rodgers is as much of an escape from reality as is her clubhouse.

Much like adolescence, the film is comical, tragic, heartbreaking, and uplifting, often in the same moment. A dream sequence toward the end of the film in which everyone Dawn knows tells her how much they love her is a reminder of how much we all want to be valued and accepted. It stresses a basic human desire that no matter how different and strange we might seem to others, we are still taken seriously and respected.

And much like real life, *Welcome to the Dollhouse* is a series of positive learning experiences. Some are embarrassing and scary while others are sweeter and more poignant. But regardless of the mood, each of these experiences is wrapped in a naïveté that we can all relate to. Throughout the story—as we cringe and laugh and shake our heads in disbelief—we want to tell Dawn that we've been there, that everything will turn out fine, that surviving junior high school is a necessary step on the path toward grasping our self-identity and becoming more autonomous.

Why You Should See This Film: Because it's a realistic representation of junior high bitterness wrapped up in mounting pessimism.

Main Themes: Jealousy * Bullying * Family * Anger * Innocence

Classic Line: "You think you're hot shit, but you're really just cold diarrhea."

Recommended Double Feature: *Pumpkin* (2002); Rated R, 117 minutes, Black comedy–drama

WHALE RIDER

(2002)

Directed by: Niki Caro
Written by: Niki Caro, based on the novel by Witi Ihimaera
Cast: Keisha Castle-Hughes (Paikea), Cliff Curtis (Porourangi), Rawiri Paratene (Koro), Vicky Haughton (Nanny Flowers), Grant Roa (Uncle Rawiri)
Rating: Rated PG-13 for brief language and a momentary drug reference
Runtime: 101 minutes
Genre: Drama

The Gist: This New Zealand film is a celebration of the human spirit. The main character, Paikea Apirana (known as Pai) is a twelve-year-old member of the Maori tribe. She dreams of someday becoming the chief, but she faces opposition from Koro, her grandfather. He believes the new leader must be a male.

The opening scenes show us tragedy as Pai's mother and twin brother die during childbirth. As these images unfold, Pai's quiet voice begins to tell us her story. First, she shares a legend passed down by her tribe and then explains that no one was happy when she was born because everyone expected her brother to lead the tribe. These deaths create a problem for the future of the Maori tribe, as well as a separation between Pai's father and grandfather. Koro seems less concerned about the death of his son's wife and more concerned with reassuring his son that he can have another child. In this sense, Koro seems to value history and tradition more than family.

The beginning of *Whale Rider* emphasizes the power of myth and legend. Pai's consistent voice-over demonstrates the importance of telling stories, and how we often tell ourselves stories to help us better understand ourselves and our place in the world. As a young girl—especially one who struggles to prove herself amid hard times and family drama—Pai attempts to show Koro that she can be a strong leader. This, however, turns out to be a difficult task considering that he blames his granddaughter for the tribe's hard times. In one of the film's more poignant scenes, her father explains that Koro wants a leader for the tribe, but "you can't just decide who those people are just because you want them to be." While Koro clearly loves Pai, he has difficulty expressing it, impeded by his own biases and cultural expectations.

The fractured family dynamics are the core of the film, and Pai tells her own story not to place blame on others, but to empathize with those around her as she tries to understand the reasoning for their actions. As Pai undergoes the transformation from a child into an adolescent, her

Keisha Castle-Hughes, Rawiri Paratene. ***Newmarket Films/Photofest © Newmarket Films. Photographer: Kirsty Griffin***

actions and emotions veer wildly from day to day. She exhibits anger, sadness, pride, and optimism. She questions her role in the village, as well as how she can break tradition while still embracing the tribe's values.

Since the death of Pai's brother and mother, her father has been absent from the village, choosing to live in Europe. He visits often and even offers to take Pai with him. The assumption is that he left the village because Koro kept pressuring him to become a leader. For teenagers, these family dynamics can resonate in positive and negative ways. Many high schoolers constantly hear about what they should do with their lives, where they should live, and what kind of person they should choose for their relationships. No one likes to have the power of choice removed, and so we empathize with both Pai and her father because we know they didn't ask for their situation, nor do they deserve it.

On the beach near her house is a *waka* (Maori canoe) that once belonged to her father. The *waka* becomes an important symbol in the film, and it is closely connected to Pai, suggesting that both of them are still being formed, waiting to be shaped properly so people in the village can appreciate their significance. The *waka* sits alone on the beach, not fulfilling its true purpose of skimming across the ocean. In much the same way, Pai feels that she is waiting in the shadows, treated unfairly because she is a female. She is preparing for the day when she can reveal her strength and earn the respect of her village. And when Koro decides it's time to gather all the boys in the village and teach them the old ways, Pai secretly watches the training sessions, studying the moves and learning the necessary songs. With the help of her uncle, she becomes more agile and skilled with the *taiha* (a traditional Maori weapon). She exhibits stoicism and self-confidence, two important qualities of any great leader.

For anyone who has ever felt pressured to assume a different identity—or to act a certain way to please someone else—*Whale Rider* is a testament to the power of staying true to oneself. It is reaffirming and inspirational, breaking down gender barriers and presenting a young girl as the hero. Adolescents want to be taken seriously by their peers, as well as by their parents and teachers, and so they relate easily to Pai's struggles. They relate to her family conflicts, namely being recognized and judged for who you are, not for who you should be or for who people expect you to be.

Pai reminds us that sometimes you have to stand tall and ignore all the negative energy that's directed at you. Sometimes, you have to dive down into the deepest part of yourself and find the courage to move forward.

Why You Should See This Film: Because it's an uplifting display of courage and determination in the face of tribal oppression.

Main Themes: Family * Empowerment * Leadership * Perseverance * Oppression

Classic Line: "In the old days, the land felt a great emptiness. It was waiting. Waiting to be filled up. Waiting for someone to love it. Waiting for a leader."

Recommended Double Feature: *Tanna* (2015); Not Rated, 104 minutes, Drama-romance

APPENDIX A
Main Themes

The sixty coming-of-age films explored in this book represent a wide range of topics and ideas. For those who like their films grouped into thematic categories, the following lists will prove useful. However, they are not exhaustive. Instead, they present a multitude of important themes that appear across a range of films. Therefore, these lists should be viewed more as a starting point for spirited and rewarding discussions.

While these various themes feature prominently in several films, how they are addressed differs greatly. A specific theme in one film might illustrate a character's strength; in another film that same theme might highlight a character's weakness. Likewise, a film from 1960 might interpret a theme much differently than a film from 2010. Themes are like chameleons. They can change their shape depending on factors such as genre, culture, gender, or even story line.

Acceptance

- *Eighth Grade*
- *Lucas*
- *Me and Earl and the Dying Girl*
- *A Monster Calls*
- *Napoleon Dynamite*
- *Orange County*
- *The Perks of Being a Wallflower*

- *Princess Cyd*
- *Sixteen Candles*
- *To All the Boys I've Loved Before*

Ambition

- *Almost Famous*
- *American Graffiti*
- *Me and Earl and the Dying Girl*
- *Saint Ralph*
- *Say Anything*
- *Sing Street*

Anger

- *Christine*
- *Igby Goes Down*
- *Lady Bird*
- *A Monster Calls*
- *Spider-Man: Homecoming*
- *Welcome to the Dollhouse*

Apathy

- *Clueless*
- *The Last Picture Show*
- *Me and Earl and the Dying Girl*
- *Napoleon Dynamite*
- *Scott Pilgrim vs. the World*

Authority

- *Ferris Bueller's Day Off*
- *Flirting*
- *Saint Ralph*
- *Sing Street*
- *The Way Way Back*

Bullying

- *The Babysitter*
- *The Breakfast Club*
- *Christine*
- *Coming through the Rye*
- *Dazed and Confused*
- *It: Chapter One*
- *Lucas*
- *My Bodyguard*
- *Rebel without a Cause*
- *Sing Street*
- *Submarine*
- *Welcome to the Dollhouse*

Class

- *Billy Elliot*
- *Igby Goes Down*
- *Pretty in Pink*
- *Say Anything*
- *Valley Girl*

Communication

- *Almost Famous*
- *Better Off Dead*
- *Call Me by Your Name*
- *Coming through the Rye*
- *The Edge of Seventeen*
- *Fast Times at Ridgemont High*
- *Lady Bird*
- *Love, Simon*
- *My Bodyguard*
- *Pretty in Pink*
- *Princess Cyd*
- *Scott Pilgrim vs. the World*

- *The Spectacular Now*
- *Submarine*
- *To All the Boys I've Loved Before*

Conformity

- *Dazed and Confused*
- *Easy A*
- *Flirting*
- *Mean Girls*

Courage

- *The Babysitter*
- *The Breadwinner*
- *Call Me by Your Name*
- *Coraline*
- *Dazed and Confused*
- *Love, Simon*
- *Moana*
- *Monster House*
- *The Perks of Being a Wallflower*
- *Saint Ralph*
- *Spider-Man: Homecoming*
- *Superbad*
- *To All the Boys I've Loved Before*

Death

- *Coming through the Rye*
- *Heathers*
- *Me and Earl and the Dying Girl*
- *A Monster Calls*
- *Stand by Me*
- *Submarine*

Deception

- *American Pie*
- *Coraline*
- *Ferris Bueller's Day Off*
- *Love, Simon*
- *Risky Business*

Depression

- *The Edge of Seventeen*
- *Ferris Bueller's Day Off*
- *Heathers*
- *Submarine*

Disillusionment

- *American Graffiti*
- *Better Off Dead*
- *Heathers*
- *The Last Picture Show*
- *Orange County*
- *Rushmore*

Empathy

- *Flirting*
- *Monster House*
- *Stand by Me*

Empowerment

- *The Breakfast Club*
- *Easy A*
- *Moana*
- *My Bodyguard*
- *Whale Rider*

Family

- *Almost Famous*
- *Billy Elliot*
- *The Breadwinner*
- *Coraline*
- *The Edge of Seventeen*
- *Hunt for the Wilderpeople*
- *Lady Bird*
- *Napoleon Dynamite*
- *Orange County*
- *Raising Victor Vargas*
- *Rebel without a Cause*
- *Sing Street*
- *The Spectacular Now*
- *Stand by Me*
- *The Way Way Back*
- *Welcome to the Dollhouse*
- *Whale Rider*

Fear

- *American Graffiti*
- *Christine*
- *It: Chapter One*
- *Love, Simon*
- *A Monster Calls*
- *Monster House*
- *The Spectacular Now*

Friendship

- *American Pie*
- *Hunt for the Wilderpeople*
- *Lucas*

- *My Bodyguard*
- *The Perks of Being a Wallflower*
- *Stand by Me*
- *Superbad*

Grief

- *Call Me by Your Name*
- *It: Chapter One*
- *My Bodyguard*
- *The Perks of Being a Wallflower*
- *Princess Cyd*
- *Saint Ralph*

Guilt

- *The Last Picture Show*
- *A Monster Calls*
- *Risky Business*
- *The Spectacular Now*

Heroism

- *Monster House*
- *Scott Pilgrim vs. the World*
- *Spider-Man: Homecoming*

Honesty

- *Call Me by Your Name*
- *Easy A*
- *Raising Victor Vargas*
- *Rebel without a Cause*
- *Say Anything*
- *To All the Boys I've Loved Before*

Individuality

- *American Graffiti*
- *The Breakfast Club*
- *Dazed and Confused*
- *Fast Times at Ridgemont High*
- *Juno*

Innocence

- *The Babysitter*
- *Fast Times at Ridgemont High*
- *It: Chapter One*
- *Welcome to the Dollhouse*

Insecurity

- *American Pie*
- *Eighth Grade*
- *Mean Girls*
- *Raising Victor Vargas*
- *Say Anything*
- *Sixteen Candles*
- *The Way Way Back*

Jealousy

- *Almost Famous*
- *Christine*
- *Coming through the Rye*
- *Lucas*
- *Mean Girls*
- *Pretty in Pink*
- *Rushmore*
- *Scott Pilgrim vs. the World*
- *Superbad*
- *Welcome to the Dollhouse*

Judgment

- *Easy A*
- *Fast Times at Ridgemont High*
- *Juno*
- *Mean Girls*
- *Valley Girl*

Leadership

- *Moana*
- *Rushmore*
- *Whale Rider*

Love

- *Better Off Dead*
- *Eighth Grade*
- *Princess Cyd*
- *Rushmore*

Naïveté

- *Clueless*
- *Juno*
- *The Last Picture Show*

Neglect

- *The Spectacular Now*
- *Stand by Me*
- *The Way Way Back*

Obsession

- *Christine*
- *Clueless*

- *Eighth Grade*
- *Heathers*

Oppression

- *Coraline*
- *Ready Player One*
- *Rebel without a Cause*
- *Whale Rider*

Peer Pressure

- *American Pie*
- *The Breakfast Club*
- *Easy A*
- *Valley Girl*

Perseverance

- *Better Off Dead*
- *Billy Elliot*
- *Lucas*
- *Ready Player One*
- *Saint Ralph*
- *Sixteen Candles*
- *Valley Girl*
- *Whale Rider*

Power

- *The Breadwinner*
- *Heathers*
- *Spider-Man: Homecoming*

Prejudice

- *Billy Elliot*
- *Love, Simon*
- *Pretty in Pink*

Pretentiousness

- *Clueless*
- *Mean Girls*
- *Scott Pilgrim vs. the World*
- *Sixteen Candles*
- *Valley Girl*

Rebelliousness

- *The Breakfast Club*
- *Coming through the Rye*
- *Dazed and Confused*
- *The Edge of Seventeen*
- *Ferris Bueller's Day Off*
- *Flirting*
- *Igby Goes Down*
- *Juno*
- *Lady Bird*
- *Rebel without a Cause*

Responsibility

- *Billy Elliot*
- *Fast Times at Ridgemont High*
- *Juno*
- *Napoleon Dynamite*
- *Raising Victor Vargas*
- *Risky Business*
- *Spider-Man: Homecoming*
- *The Way Way Back*

Self-Awareness

- *The Babysitter*
- *Moana*
- *Orange County*
- *Raising Victor Vargas*
- *Sing Street*

Self-Confidence

- *Better Off Dead*
- *Eighth Grade*
- *Ferris Bueller's Day Off*
- *Me and Earl and the Dying Girl*
- *Napoleon Dynamite*
- *The Perks of Being a Wallflower*
- *To All the Boys I've Loved Before*

Selfishness

- *Almost Famous*
- *American Graffiti*
- *American Pie*
- *Clueless*
- *The Edge of Seventeen*
- *Igby Goes Down*
- *Pretty in Pink*
- *Superbad*

Sexual Discovery

- *Call Me by Your Name*
- *Flirting*
- *Lady Bird*
- *The Last Picture Show*
- *Princess Cyd*
- *Risky Business*

- *Submarine*
- *Superbad*

Survival

- *The Babysitter*
- *The Breadwinner*
- *Coraline*
- *Hunt for the Wilderpeople*
- *Igby Goes Down*
- *Ready Player One*
- *Spider-Man: Homecoming*

Teamwork

- *Hunt for the Wilderpeople*
- *It: Chapter One*
- *Monster House*
- *Orange County*
- *Ready Player One*
- *Risky Business*

Trust

- *Hunt for the Wilderpeople*
- *Moana*
- *Say Anything*
- *Sixteen Candles*

War

- *The Breadwinner*
- *Ready Player One*
- *Rushmore*

APPENDIX B
Genres

Just like there are multiple cliques roaming the high school hallways, so, too, are there numerous genres roaming the cinematic landscape. The lists below are a breakdown of the genres included in this book. Given the conflicting emotions that highlight the coming-of-age years—especially the potent mixture of humor and pathos—many of the sixty films discussed in this book represent more than one genre. While comedy and drama appear regularly, there are other genres that prove just as interesting and important when applied to adolescence.

Our personal attraction to a specific genre often depends on our interests and personality. We tend to gravitate toward those films that best embody either our own moods and desires, or our own anxieties and fears. There's a comfort level in viewing those films, as if we're being included in a group of friends who know us well. There are times, however, when we feel like taking a risk and venturing into uncharted waters.

Action and Adventure

- *Hunt for the Wilderpeople*
- *Moana*
- *Ready Player One*
- *Scott Pilgrim vs. the World*
- *Spider-Man: Homecoming*

Animation

- *The Breadwinner*
- *Coraline*
- *Moana*
- *Monster House*

Comedy

- *Almost Famous*
- *American Graffiti*
- *American Pie*
- *The Babysitter*
- *Better Off Dead*
- *Billy Elliot*
- *The Breakfast Club*
- *Clueless*
- *Dazed and Confused*
- *Easy A*
- *The Edge of Seventeen*
- *Fast Times at Ridgemont High*
- *Ferris Bueller's Day Off*
- *Heathers*
- *Hunt for the Wilderpeople*
- *Igby Goes Down*
- *Juno*
- *Lady Bird*
- *Love, Simon*
- *Lucas*
- *Me and Earl and the Dying Girl*
- *Mean Girls*
- *Napoleon Dynamite*
- *Orange County*
- *Pretty in Pink*
- *Risky Business*
- *Rushmore*
- *Saint Ralph*

- *Say Anything*
- *Sing Street*
- *Sixteen Candles*
- *Submarine*
- *Superbad*
- *To All the Boys I've Loved Before*
- *Valley Girl*
- *The Way Way Back*
- *Welcome to the Dollhouse*

Drama

- *Almost Famous*
- *American Graffiti*
- *Billy Elliot*
- *The Breadwinner*
- *The Breakfast Club*
- *Call Me by Your Name*
- *Coming through the Rye*
- *The Edge of Seventeen*
- *Eighth Grade*
- *Fast Times at Ridgemont High*
- *Flirting*
- *Hunt for the Wilderpeople*
- *Igby Goes Down*
- *Juno*
- *Lady Bird*
- *Love, Simon*
- *Lucas*
- *Me and Earl and the Dying Girl*
- *A Monster Calls*
- *My Bodyguard*
- *The Perks of Being a Wallflower*
- *Princess Cyd*
- *Raising Victor Vargas*
- *Rebel without a Cause*
- *Risky Business*

- *Rushmore*
- *Saint Ralph*
- *Say Anything*
- *Sing Street*
- *The Spectacular Now*
- *Stand by Me*
- *Submarine*
- *The Way Way Back*
- *Welcome to the Dollhouse*
- *Whale Rider*

Fantasy

- *Coraline*
- *A Monster Calls*
- *Monster House*
- *Scott Pilgrim vs. the World*

Horror

- *The Babysitter*
- *Christine*
- *Coraline*
- *It: Chapter One*
- *Monster House*

Romance

- *Call Me by Your Name*
- *Easy A*
- *Flirting*
- *Love, Simon*
- *Lucas*
- *Pretty in Pink*
- *Princess Cyd*
- *Raising Victor Vargas*
- *Say Anything*

- *Sixteen Candles*
- *The Spectacular Now*
- *Submarine*
- *To All the Boys I've Loved Before*
- *Valley Girl*

Science Fiction

- *Ready Player One*

APPENDIX C
Top-Five Lists

We often classify films by genre and theme, or by social factors such as language, nudity, and violence. Sometimes, though, it's fun to be creative. Sometimes, we want to organize the films we love on a more eclectic scale. Part of the reason we enjoy making lists is because they are entirely subjective. They make a definitive statement with which others will undoubtedly disagree.

The top-five lists included below represent those groupings most interesting and beneficial for those with a fondness for coming-of-age films. Certainly, there are several other films in this book that could be included on each one of these lists, and many of you will be quite vocal in expressing your opinion.

As you read through this book—and as you watch the films—consider creating your own lists. Share them with your friends. Argue about whether or not they deserve to be included. You will often find that in discussing how and why you created such a list, you will come to a better understanding of the various ways those films are important to you personally.

Best Best Friends

- *Ferris Bueller's Day Off*
- *It: Chapter One*
- *Monster House*

- *Sing Street*
- *Stand by Me*

Best Coming-of-Age Post High School

- *Adventureland* (2009)
- *The Graduate* (1967)
- *High Fidelity* (2000)
- *Swingers* (1996)
- *The World's End* (2013)

Best Soundtrack

- *Almost Famous*
- *American Graffiti*
- *Dazed and Confused*
- *Pretty in Pink*
- *Sing Street*

Best Tearjerker

- *Me and Earl and the Dying Girl*
- *A Monster Calls*
- *The Perks of Being a Wallflower*
- *Stand by Me*
- *Whale Rider*

Best to Watch after a Breakup

- *Christine*
- *Heathers*
- *Ready Player One*
- *Scott Pilgrim vs. the World*
- *The Spectacular Now*

Best to Watch with Parents

- *Hunt for the Wilderpeople*
- *Moana*
- *My Bodyguard*
- *Spider-Man: Homecoming*
- *Whale Rider*

Coolest Parents

- *Call Me by Your Name*
- *Easy A*
- *Juno*
- *Love, Simon*
- *To All the Boys I've Loved Before*

Funniest

- *American Pie*
- *Clueless*
- *Orange County*
- *Rushmore*
- *Superbad*

Honorable Mentions

- *City of God* (2002)
- *George Washington* (2000)
- *Leolo* (1992)
- *Liberty Heights* (1999)
- *Mud* (2012)

Most Awkward

- *Eighth Grade*
- *Napoleon Dynamite*
- *Submarine*

- *The Way Way Back*
- *Welcome to the Dollhouse*

Most Diverse

- *The Breadwinner*
- *Flirting*
- *Love, Simon*
- *Raising Victor Vargas*
- *Whale Rider*

Most Rebellious

- *The Edge of Seventeen*
- *Ferris Bueller's Day Off*
- *Igby Goes Down*
- *Lady Bird*
- *Rebel without a Cause*

Most Romantic

- *Pretty in Pink*
- *Princess Cyd*
- *Say Anything*
- *Sixteen Candles*
- *Valley Girl*

Most Uplifting

- *Billy Elliot*
- *Hunt for the Wilderpeople*
- *Lucas*
- *Saint Ralph*
- *Whale Rider*

Toughest Breakups

- *Better Off Dead*
- *Igby Goes Down*
- *The Last Picture Show*
- *Say Anything*
- *Valley Girl*

Worst to Watch with Parents

- *American Pie*
- *Dazed and Confused*
- *Fast Times at Ridgemont High*
- *Risky Business*
- *Superbad*

INDEX

Note: Bold page numbers indicate photos.

ABOUT THE AUTHOR

Michael Howarth received his bachelor's degree in English from James Madison University and an MFA in creative writing from the University of Alaska Anchorage. Following his MFA, he attended the University of Louisiana Lafayette, where he completed his PhD in literary and cultural studies. He is currently a professor of English at Missouri Southern State University, where he teaches children's literature and film studies in addition to directing the honors program. His critical text *Under the Bed, Creeping: Psychoanalyzing the Gothic in Children's Literature* was published in 2014. His young adult novel *Fair Weather Ninjas* was published in 2016.

www.ingramcontent.com/pod-product-compliance
Lightning Source LLC
Chambersburg PA
CBHW030310100426
42812CB00002B/648

9781538120019